CHANGE OF NAME
AND
LAW OF NAMES

Legal Almanac Series No. 34

CHANGE OF NAME
AND
LAW OF NAMES

by   Edward J. Bander

1973
OCEANA PUBLICATIONS, INC.
Dobbs Ferry, New York

This is a revised and updated edition of How to Change Your Name and the Law of Names by Lawrence G. Greene, the thirty-fourth number in a series of LEGAL ALMANACS which bring you the law on various subjects in nontechnical language. These books do not take the place of your attorney's advice, but they can introduce you to your legal rights and responsibilities.

Library of Congress Cataloging in Publication Data

Bander, Edward J.
    Change of name and law of names.

    (Legal almanac series, no. 34)
    "Revised and updated edition of How to change your
name, and the law of names, by Lawrence G. Greene."
        Bibliography: p.
        1. Names, Personal -- United States -- Law. I. Greene,
Lawrence Gerard. How to change your name, and the
law of names. II. Title
KF468.Z9G7   1973   346'.73'012   73-11060
ISBN   0-379-11088-1

This edition is dedicated to my sister, Mrs. Natalie Davis, who has always encouraged me to make a name for myself.

Manufactured in the United States of America

TABLE OF CONTENTS

Preface   v

Chapter 1 CHANGING YOUR NAME   1

Chapter 2 THE STATUTORY WAY   5
   Where the Application is Made   7
   Publication Requirements   7
   Residence Requirements   8
   Children   8
   Aliens 12
   Birth Records 13
   Change of Sex 13
   Homosexuals 14
   Adoption Proceedings 14
   Resumption of Name by a Divorcee 14

Chapter 3 MOTIVES AND PURPOSES BEHIND THE CHANGE 17

Chapter 4 THE USE AND ABUSE OF NAMES 25

Chapter 5 FICTITIOUS AND ASSUMED NAMES 28
   Conducting Business Under an Assumed Name 30

Chapter 6 YOUR NAME AND YOUR IDENTITY 34
   Legal Documents 34
   Middle Names and Initials 38
   Defamation 41
   Idem Sonans 42

Chapter 7 THE MARRIED WOMAN AND HER NAME 45

Chapter 8 BUSINESS NAMES 60

Appendix A SUMMARY OF STATE LAWS RELATING TO CHANGE
          OF NAME 65

Appendix B FORMS 81
   Petition for Change of Name 81
   Petition for Change of Name of Infant 85
   Notice of Petition to Change Name of Infant 89
   Order Changing Name; General Form 91
   Order Changing Name; Directing Change of Name of Infant 95
   Certificate of Compliance with Order for Change of Name 97

Appendix C COMMON LAW Alice W. Smith v. United States
            Casualty Company.   98

Appendix D CASE CITATIONS.   104

Appendix E MAIDEN NAME BILLS   106

Appendix F BIBLIOGRAPHY   111

Index   115

PREFACE

The author would like to extend his thanks to
the students in his introductory seminar course at
New York University School of Law and his para-
legal course at the School of Continuing Education
at New York University for their willingness to
accept problems related to my editing of this book.
He would also like to thank Ms. Lida Bander for
her extensive help in the checking, researching
and typing of this manuscript; and also Mrs. Frances
W. Bander for her editing of the chapter on married
women. The author would like to think that all the
comments he has added to this book are his own.

Chapter 1

CHANGING YOUR NAME

If you desire to change your name you may do so, in practically every state, without making an application to any court for permission to adopt the new name. This was also the rule at the common law, and is qualified only by the condition that there be no criminal or fraudulent intent behind the proposed change.

But while the change of name may be almost everywhere effected without a court decree, provision is also made universally for a means by which a new name may be formally adopted. This procedure, which is statutory and must be followed strictly, involves the submission of a petition to the appropriate court and the granting of the petition by a formal order.

In some states, the law may require that a hearing be held so that interested persons may have an opportunity to appear and interpose objections to the proposed change. Of course, the courts will not entertain frivolous objections, and only if the objections are substantial and meritorious will they be given serious consideration. Such objections are comparatively rare, and the course of the usual court proceeding is smooth and uneventful.

In the pages that follow we will examine the statutory requirements in detail in a manner which we trust will be interesting to the general reader.

The law relating to names, their significance, and their change, has its origin in the dim past, a past when a person bore only one name, which was sufficient in a primitive society to identify him and distinguish him from his fellow men. Names were derived from many diverse sources. (See Appendix C for a scholarly opinion on the origin of names.) A name might have attached itself to an individual quite naturally from the place in which he resided, or the occupation he pursued. Or, again, names might find their source in the names of animals, or in superstitious hopes or fears. Thus we find that a person's family name had a special significance when first used.

With the passage of time, however, and the consequent complication of society, we find the Christian or "given" name used in conjunction with the family name or "surname." At first the given name, being the name given at baptism, was the only name of importance. Then the surname, a kind of qualification or description, came into wide-spread use together with that given at birth. Until comparatively late in legal history, important documents were still signed only with the given name, and legal proceedings could be conducted only in the one given name. For example, in the yearbooks of Edward I we find the following recorded:

> "One Matthew came to the market at B. and found in the hands of one Robert his horse, which had been the night before stolen from his house in the town of T., and that he raised the cry on the said Robert, and so both man and horse were taken."

Or the following, taken from the yearbooks of Edward II:

> "A certain Alice appealed one John of rape and breach of the peace of our Lord and King. . . . John came and defended all manner of felony . . . and . . . if Alice, by advice of counsel, had not withdrawn her appeal, the judgment of the Court would have been that Alice should tear out John's eyes, etc."

It also became customary for a man to add to his given name that of his father, so that, if his Christian name were John, and his father's name were Patrick, he might be called John Fitzpatrick, the prefix "fitz" being equivalent to the French "fils" or "son."

With time, the surname became hereditary, and we find the appearance of the family name, continuing from father to son from one generation to another.

So important was the baptismal name, that it could not be changed, nor could a person, having once been baptized, be later baptized with an additional name, but it has been said that today, because of the diversity of sects, there is a possibility of more than one baptism which may take place when a person enters a different sect.

We may say that a name is a designation used to identify or distinguish one individual from another. That is the essential purpose of a name, whether, as in ancient times, it consisted of a given name only, or of a family name in addition, derived from a person's parents.

Today, the laws of England and of the United States provide that both given and surnames may be adopted or changed by a person in later life, and it is with such changes, and how they may be effected, that this book is in great part concerned.

At common law, that is, the unwritten law of the courts as distinguished from statutory law, or the law embodied in the acts of a legislature, the right to change one's name without legal proceedings was eventually fully recognized. This common law right was not changed or abrogated by statutes which provided a legal procedure for such change, unless, of course, the statute specifically removed such right. Therefore, unless the statutory method is exclusive, the common law rule is in no way affected.

Under the common law rule, where it is not done for an illegal or fraudulent purpose, an individual may lawfully adopt any name without seeking a court's permission to do so or resorting to any other legal proceeding. When a name is adopted in this manner, it becomes for all purposes the individual's legal name. There is no reason why a person may not change his name as often as he chooses, provided, as indicated above, no criminal or other improper intention is behind the assumption of the new name.

But, in spite of the general principle, one should exercise some care in assuming and acting under a new name, since legal complications may sometimes arise. For example, in California, a court has decided that where a person signs an affidavit of registration as an elector, and states therein a name which is different from that of his birth and which is different from the name he used on passports and other federal matters, he may be convicted of perjury. Such conviction was sustained even though the name used in the affidavit was always used by the person in the state and although he was married under such name. (59 Cal. App. (2) 342, 139 P. (2) 118)

Although the common law rule prevails generally in the United States, many persons follow the statutory proceeding to change their names simply to have, wherever possible, a record of the change.

As will be seen hereafter, the court to which a petition for leave to assume a new name has been presented may generally, in its discretion, refuse to grant the application. However, if it appears that the court's discretion has been abused in refusing to recognize the petition, or that the court acted in an

3

arbitrary manner, then the court's action may be subject to review and correction by an appellate court.

What circumstances will or will not justify a court's refusal to entertain a petition for change of name is difficult to predict. Every case turns on its own facts. In any case, a person desiring to change his or her name will be well advised to consult an attorney and not attempt to prepare the necessary papers without legal counsel.

Chapter 2

THE STATUTORY WAY

While, as we have already said, you may change your name with perfect propriety without resorting to court or other legal proceedings, nevertheless you may have reasons to change your name by following the statutory procedure which your state provides. The main reason for following this method is so that the change will be a matter of record. However, you should keep in mind the fact that once you have changed your name in this manner, you will probably be unable to assume any name thereafter unless you again pursue the same formal procedure.

You will find in Appendix A of this book a summary of the statutory provisions on this subject, for each of the fifty states and for the District of Columbia. You will also note that while there is some difference in detail the procedure generally is to file a petition, application or declaration, with a court or public officer, stating the name to be newly taken, and the reasons for such change. In some states the petition must be published in a newspaper and hearings may be held at which any interested person may appear and interpose objections. If any objections are made, the court may set the matter down for a hearing and take testimony. As a result of the hearing the court may dismiss the objections and grant the petition, or may sustain the objections and refuse to permit the requested change.

We have said that the common law procedure permits a person to change his name without formal legal proceedings. Even where statutes provide a formal method, the common law way is not generally abrogated. However, in some states the statutes are so worded as to imply that the only way to change one's name is by following the statute. For example, in Pennsylvania the statute on the subject specifically states that it is unlawful to assume a different name except by court proceedings, and the Oklahoma statute indicates that the statutory remedy is exclusive, that no change of name will be permitted except as provided by the statute, or by marriage, decree of divorce or adoption. In these states a person desiring to change his name should seek the advice of an attorney and follow that statute.

In some jurisdictions, e.g., Iowa and North Carolina, only

one change may be permitted under the statute, although North Carolina law permits a petitioner to resume his former name on application.

Some states are most detailed in the procedure to be followed, while others dispose of the subject in a sentence or two. New York, for example, has a statute which covers the matter at considerable length, while Alabama and Mississippi have very brief laws on the subject.

A number of states provide that an unlawful change of name, or a change made for criminal or fraudulent purposes, is a crime, punishable as a misdemeanor. This is one additional reason, if further reason is needed, why an attorney should be consulted when a change of name is contemplated.

The statute of Minnesota and some other states require that the petition for change of name describe the real property which the petitioner owns or in which he has an interest, or with respect to which he has any liens, mortgages, etc.

The state constitutions of many states prohibit the enactment of special legislation or local laws which change the names of individuals. This simply means that the state legislature may not pass a statute which changes the name of an individual. Of course, a person may still follow the statutory procedure or the common law procedure, if the latter method has not been abrogated.

It is of the highest importance that the information contained in the petition be accurate in every respect. The courts look with disfavor upon a petition which is carelessly drawn, vague or inaccurate. When you consult an attorney in this matter, you should be certain that you give him all the information he desires and that the information so given be correct in all details. Otherwise, the court may dismiss the petition, which may preclude you from getting the relief at any time in the future in that state, or, at best, may mean the loss of time and trouble involved in preparing a new petition to the court's satisfaction.

In one case, the petition stated that the petitioner had registered a trade name which was the name the petitioner desired to adopt. As a matter of fact, the name had never been registered as alleged. This may have been the result of a careless oversight and no willful falsehood was intended. However, the court said that the representation was a material one, and because of its falsity the court felt constrained to vacate a previous order which had allowed the change of name. (95 N.Y.S. (2) 783) It is possible that the petition would have been granted if no reference had been made to the alleged registration, but once the statement was made, it had to be accurate.

A petition and order for change of name in the state of New York are set forth in Appendix B.

WHERE THE APPLICATION IS MADE

In our discussion of the statutory procedure we have frequently referred to the court as the authority which has the power of granting the petition to change one's name. But while, in fact, it is a court of record which authorizes the change in a majority of the states, some statutes provide that the authorization may be granted by a different public official.

In the state of Iowa, it seems that the person desiring to change his or her name files a statement to that effect with the clerk of the District Court. In North Carolina the application is filed before the clerk of the Superior Court and the order of change is issued by the clerk.

The particular court or official to whom the petition is presented is, of course, specified by the statute. The court may be the Probate or Surrogate's Court, the Superior Court, the Chancery Court, or whatever other tribunal is designated. In any case, it is generally required that the court to which the application is made be located in the county, district or parish (in the case of Louisiana), of the applicant's residence.

PUBLICATION REQUIREMENTS

A number of states require that the petition for the change of name, notice of hearing, or the final decree of the court granting the change be published in a newspaper for a stated period. The jurisdictions requiring such publication seem to be Colorado, Delaware, District of Columbia, Georgia, Hawaii, Idaho, Illinois, Indiana, Kansas, Michigan, Missouri, Montana, Nebraska, Nevada, New Mexico, New York, North Dakota, Ohio, Oklahoma, Pennsylvania, South Dakota, Vermont, West Virginia, Wisconsin.

The statutes of Arizona and Utah provide that the appropriate court "may" order publication or notice of hearing. Maine, Massachusetts, Oregon and Wyoming require that public notice be given, presumably by publication in the same way as other legal notices are published. The North Carolina statute requires that the notice be published at the "courthouse door."

For the duration of such publication in the various jurisdictions where required, the reader is referred to Appendix A, where the state requirements are set forth in more detail.

Where the application of a name change (from Malcolm Whyte to Youssouph Diallo) requested in forma pauperis, and the cost of publication was to be assumed by the local government, it was essential to give notice to the city finance administrator. (N.Y.L.J., Nov. 9, 1972, p. 1.)

RESIDENCE REQUIREMENTS

The statutes often require that the person applying for a change of name be a resident of the state or county, or both, for a specified period of time. However, this requirement is not universal, as the reader will see by an inspection of the laws on this subject gathered in Appendix A.

The fact of residence is itself almost everywhere a requisite, whatever the time element may be, although, for example in the state of Alabama, the statute may even be silent on this point.

A number of states are silent on the length of such residence; other states may require that the petitioner reside in the county for one year before filing the application (Michigan, Minnesota, Nebraska, Ohio, Utah, West Virginia); in North Dakota and South Dakota, the period is six months; in Oklahoma the applicant must be domiciled in the state for three years and in the county for at least thirty days; in Pennsylvania the petitioner must set forth his residences for the preceeding five years, while in Wyoming the residence requirement is two years.

If the statute is silent on the question of length of residence, the court to whom the petition is presented may not of its own accord arbitrarily establish a period of time. In two cases, the court refused to grant a petition to change a name where the petitioners did not reside in the state for one year, although no period of any kind was required by the statute. The petitioners appealed from this ruling and the appellate court sustained the position of the petitioners, stating that only the legislature may fix a period of residence and that it was an abuse of the court's power to do so. (97 Cal. App. (2) 838, 218 P. (2) 784; 101 Cal. App. (2) 70, 224 P. (2) 911)

CHILDREN

A child, as well as an adult, may have his name changed

by following the statutory formalities. However, the petition of a minor for change of name must be signed by the parents or surviving parent, guardian or next friend of the infant. An infant is, in the eyes of the law, a person under the age of twenty-one years, except in states, such as New Jersey, that have lowered the age to eighteen.

The statutes generally require that if the child is over a specified age, fourteen years or sixteen years, he must also join in the petition.

It has been noted that the courts have discretion whether or not to grant an application for change of name. This is especially true in the case of infants, and if it should appear to the court that the best interests of the child would be served by allowing the application it will be granted. However, if the child's welfare would be adversely affected by the change, then the court will probably refuse to entertain the petition. The New York statute on the subject specifically provides that the court will order the change of an infant's name if it appears to the court's satisfaction that the interests of the infant will be "substantially promoted."

Even if the parents are separated, the court may hold that the consent of both is necessary, where such consent is made a requisite by the statute. (19 N.Y.S. (2) 839)

However, if one of the parents is unable to join in the petition for reason of incompetency, absence from the country, or because the parent is imprisoned, the courts will probably accept the petition of one parent.

In one case, an application was made by a boy sixteen years old, together with his mother, for leave to assume the name of his stepfather. His parents were divorced and the mother has been given custody of the child. The boy had been known by his stepfather's name for several years prior to the application and saw his father, who has also remarried, only at rare intervals. The court noted the absence of a close filial relationship between the boy and his natural father, and denied the father's objections to the proposed change. (21 N.Y.S. (2) 453) In an interesting case allowing a change of name from that of the putative father, followed by a reversal in an intermediate appellate court, and a reversal of that court by the highest court of Texas, it was determined that the natural father's rights are subservient to the best interests of the child. Although the natural father had been guilty of no misconduct and the court sympathized with his desire that his son bear his name, the court nevertheless held: (1) that there is no property right in a child's name and thus no violation of the due processclause of the Fourteenth Amendment to the U.S. Constitution nor of any provision of the state constitution to grant the change of name; and (2) the fact that the child had been known by his stepfather's name from the age of two was one of many significant factors that precluded any reversal of the trial judge's decision for abuse of discretion. (433 SW (2) 420) Cases of this type are rather frequent, the child taking the name of his stepfather or, if his mother has not remarried, her maiden name.

Sometimes, however, a court will refuse to permit an infant to change his name over the objections of the father. (216 La. 241, 43 So. (2) 595)* In another case, a divorced wife, who had guardianship of her infant children, still of tender age, had remarried and had given the children the surname of her new husband. This was done without seeking the permission of a court. Her former husband was successful in obtaining a court order restraining the mother from changing the infants' names without further order of the court. The court pointed out that the infants, even though their mother had remarried, remained members of their father's family. (50 N.Y.S. (2) 278) It has also been said that the father has a "primary right to have his children bear his name." (57 N.Y.S. (2) 283)

The divorced mother who has custody of an infant child will quite naturally desire that the child take the name of the person whom she remarries. As has been noted, however, the courts may be reluctant to allow such change over the objections of the child's natural father. It is not necessarily in the best interests of the child that he be called by the name of his mother's new husband. The courts seek at all times to make their determination in such cases serve the interests of the infant, considering all the surrounding circumstances. The courts are especially reluctant to damage or, in some cases, destroy the already tenuous and delicate relation which exists between the child of divorced parents and its natural parent. The use of an injunction was permitted the father of a seven year old boy as against the mother and stepfather. (41 Del. Ch. 46, 187 A. (2) 436) On the other hand, the father's attempt to prevent the name change was denied in 124 Ga. App. 603, 184 S.E. (2) 696. What

* See also 106 N.Y.S. (2) 794, and 230 Miss. 719, 93 So (2) 822

is in the best interests of the child appears to be the paramount rule.

However, if it should appear that the divorced father is indifferent to the child's welfare, that he sees the child not at all or only at the rarest intervals and makes no effort to give the child the affection of a natural parent, then the court may well decide that the petition to change the child's name should be granted. (63 N.Y.S. (2) 83) While in most cases the name to be newly given to the child is that of the stepfather, it has occurred that the mother has not remarried but wishes the child to take her maiden name, which she herself has resumed after the divorce. The courts will give to such a request the same consideration that we have noted above, in deciding whether to allow the change. (43 N.Y.S. (2) 521)

The courts may be convinced in the particular case that it would not contribute to the child's welfare to interfere with the usual succession to the surname of the father and thus, as has been said, "to foster any unnatural barrier between father and son." It should be kept in mind that when the child arrives at more mature years he may understand the circumstances more clearly and then, if he wishes to bear another name, he may do so by following the common law procedure or by applying to the courts.

In one case, it seems that a divorced mother, who had remarried, registered her infant son in school under the name of her new husband. The natural father applied to the court for an order (called "mandamus") directing the board of education to register his son by his true name. The petition was granted. (104 N.Y.S. (2) 421) In another interesting situation, P., claiming to be the child's natural father, besought the court to direct the Department of Health to issue an amended birth certificate to show that the child's surname was the same as that of P. It seems that P. had not married the child's mother and that the mother did marry one H., whose name was borne by the child. The court denied the application in the absence of the mother's joining in the application, and especially in view of the legal presumption that the child was legitimate. (107 N.YS. (2) 586)

Sometimes the courts will construe the relevant statutes strictly, as witness the case where a mother applied to change the name of her child, who was under sixteen years of age, to that of her new husband. The natural father had been adjudged incompetent and had been committed to an institution, and a special guardian had been appointed for him. The marriage had been annulled. The special guardian, acting for the father, refused to join in the petition, and the court denied the application. The statute specifically required the consent of both parents if living. However, it was pointed out that if the present husband would adopt the child formally, then the name could be changed as requested. (118 N.Y.S. (2) 594)

It has, however, been held proper to change the name of the child to that of the divorced mother's subsequent husband where the child was known at home and at school by such name since he was one year old. (83 Ga. App. 280, 63 S.E. (2) 345) And, of course, if the consent of both parents is not required by the statute, a change of name will be allowed if in the child's interests. (220 Ark. 377, 247 S.W. (2) 1015)

Where the mother of an illegitimate child and the putative father agreed to change the name of their child to that of the putative father, the objection of the legal spouse of the putative father was not sufficient to prevent the granting of the application. The court held: "While there is a paucity of precedent on this question, it is apparent that the court has wide discretion in granting or refusing an application for a change of name. Circumstances of special significance that would militate against the granting of such an application would be an unworthy motive, the possibility of fraud on the public, or the choice of a name that is bizarre, unduly lengthy, ridiculous or offensive to common decency and good taste." (91 N.J. Super. 296, 219 A(2) 906)

We have thus far discussed mainly change of the child's name by formal court procedure. But it has happened that the daughter of divorced parents, who was under twenty-one but apparently mature, voluntarily changed her surname to that of the mother's subsequent husband. She did so by following the common law method and did not apply to any court for permission to do so. When her natural father sought to compel his daughter by court order to desist from using the name, the court refused his request and stated that even a minor can take the name he or she chooses. Of course, if the daughter had wished to change her name by court proceedings, she would have had to appear by her guardian and follow the other statutory requirements. (12 N.J. Super. 350, 79 A. (2) 497)

ALIENS

There appears to be no reason why an alien, lawfully and

properly admitted to our country, should not be permitted to effect a change in his name in the same way as a citizen, and subject to the same conditions that the requested change shall be made without any ulterior purpose. In accordance with this principle, a court has granted the petition of alien parents and their infant children, who came to this country from France fearing persecution. The parents had applied for their first papers, although the court did not stress this circumstance. In its decision the court noted that such applications by non-citizens had met with judicial refusal on the theory that aliens were not entitled to such relief. But the court also pointed out that there was no statutory bar to the desired change, and since the aliens could, in any case, change their names without court approval, it was desirable that the change be made a matter of record. (32 N.Y.S. (2) 264)

It is precisely this common law right which makes it difficult for the layman to understand why a court will refuse to grant an application for change of name, assuming, of course, that no improper motives are present. And it would seem not only proper but desirable that where an alien is concerned, the change be recorded so that the public will be advised of the fact.

BIRTH RECORDS

When a change of name has been brought about by following the statutory procedure and an order to such effect has been made by the court, the statutes sometimes require that a copy of the court order or a transcript thereof be transmitted to the bureau of vital statistics in the state, and a correction made of the birth certificate if the person was born in the particular state.

Such changes in vital statistics records are usually kept confidential and the old records may be sealed and kept from inspection by the casual public. On this matter, as, indeed, on all matters relating to this subject, the statutes of the state involved should be consulted.

CHANGE OF SEX

A transexual who has had his male organs removed and who wishes a female identity has been allowed a change of name from a male first name to a female first name. (57 Misc. (2) 813, 293 N.Y.S. (2) 834)

HOMOSEXUALS

Needless to say, homosexuals find the discretion of the judiciary overpowering in their efforts to secure an identity for themselves. A graduate of a law school, barred from openly marrying one of his sex, legally changed his name from Jack Baker to Pat McConnell, obtained a license to marry, and did indeed marry. (New York Times, Jan. 7, 1973, p. 55)

ADOPTION PROCEEDINGS

We have thus far been concerned primarily in proceedings which have for their principal purpose the change of name of an adult or a minor. However, as incidental to other types of proceedings or legal actions, a court may allow a change of name of one or more individuals if such change is deemed appropriate. In an adoption proceeding, a change of name almost invariably accompanies the adoption of the child. It has been said: ''A legal adoption is a proceeding which establishes the relationship of parent and child between persons who are not so related by nature.''*

Adoption proceedings are necessarily technical in their nature, and the assistance of competent counsel is advisable. Court hearings are held and the final result is a decree of adoption which may provide for a change of the child's name if the petition so requests.

The statutes often provide that the papers in an adoption proceeding be sealed, which means that they are not open to public inspection. Provision is also often made for the issuance of a new birth certificate in the new name of the adopted child, the original birth certificate being sealed.

RESUMPTION OF NAME BY A DIVORCEE

It would seem that under the common law principle already discussed, a divorced woman is free to assume such name as she chooses, subject, of course, to whatever limitations the state law may impose in such cases. But in a number of states, as will

* See Law of Adoption (1968) by Morton L. Leavy, Oceana Publications. An excellent discussion of state laws respecting adoption requirements and proceedings.

be seen from an inspection of the state laws summarized in Appendix A, the legislatures have incorporated in their divorce laws provisions directly bearing upon the right of a divorced woman to resume her maiden name, the name of a former husband, or any other name.

The states and other jurisdictions which have enacted statutes on this matter are the following: Alaska, Arizona, Arkansas, California, Connecticut, Delaware, District of Columbia, Georgia, Hawaii, Illinois, Indiana, Kansas, Maine, Massachusetts, Michigan, Minnesota, Missouri, Nevada, New Hampshire, New Jersey, North Carolina, Ohio, Oklahoma, Oregon, Pennsylvania, Rhode Island, South Carolina, South Dakota, Texas, Vermont, Virginia, Washington, West Virginia, Wisconsin.

In some states, it appears that the court will grant a change of name to a divorced woman if the divorce was not obtained because of her own fault. In other words, in such states the divorce must, apparently, have been obtained by the woman. The states so providing are Delaware, Kentucky, Massachusetts, Minnesota, Missouri, Oklahoma, Rhode Island, Vermont, West Virginia.

The laws of some jurisdictions further limit the woman's right to change her name to those situations in which there are no minor children of the marriage or where she is not given custody of a minor child. That is the case in Arkansas, Michigan, South Dakota, West Virginia, Wisconsin.

New Jersey specifically provides that a divorced woman may be ordered to desist from using the surname of her divorced husband.

While a divorced woman may have her problems in changing her name, they are as nothing compared to those of a married woman separated from her husband. The opinion of a lower court judge reprinted in full below typifies the arbitrariness of judges who believe the discretion allowed by law to them in statutory change of name petitions extends to imposing their "social mores" on society:

> MATTER OF ROBBINS -- This application by a married woman, who is separated from her husband pursuant to a separation agreement executed Sept. 7, 1971, for leave to assume her maiden name, is denied.
>
> Her economic standing, contrary to her allegation in the petition, will not be affected in any way. The expertise in the field of nursing, which she relates, is

resident with her and is not measured by her name. Most females receive their degrees in academic or professional pursuits in their maiden names. A single affidavit of identification is all that is necessary to demonstrate that the degree recipient is the same person as the one who relies on these achievements in applying for any kind of position.

One who is seeking to be employed in the public realm would be well advised to conform to the social mores of our times. A resumption of her maiden name, while she is still a married woman, although separated, might lead some employers to believe she is attempting a misrepresentation. Any order changing her name now would require her to carry around copies of the order to explain the situation.

The application is denied. (N.Y.L.J., Aug. 7, 1972)

In the chapter on married women we cite the instance of a Massachusetts woman who was permitted to change her name to one distinct from that of her husband. One would think that if that were acceptable, then, a fortiori, a woman separated from her husband could assume her maiden, or any other, name. Possibly, if we substitute the word "sex" for "race" in the paragraph below we can understand the fight for equality in the right to change one's name:

> "The drive to end racial [sexual] discrimination now extends beyond blatant racial [sexual] distinctions to less obvious and less intentional forms of unequal treatment; nonetheless, there still exist laws and governmental programs that are racially [sexually] neutral on their face but that may have a racially [sexually] discriminatory impact in practice." (Silverman, Equal Protection, Economic Legislation, and Racial Discrimination, 25 Vand. L.R. 1183 (1972) (material in brackets added.)

Previously we have discussed the right of a divorced wife to change the name of her minor children, of which she has custody, when the divorced husband has made objection to the proposed change, and in Chapter Seven we will treat the rights of a married woman so far as her name is concerned.

Chapter 3

MOTIVES AND PURPOSES BEHIND THE CHANGE

The statutes of the majority of states require that the petition for the change of name set forth the reasons for the change. Where this requirement appears, the petition must indicate without equivocation why the petitioner desires to make the change. The law also generally gives to the court to which the petition is submitted a wide latitude in granting or refusing to grant the petition. If, therefore, the reasons are not stated, or if they are vaguely stated, the court may deny the application. And, of course, if the reasons, though fully expressed, appear to the court to be improper, the change will not be allowed. The only states whose statutes do not seem to require a specific statement of the reasons behind the proposed change are Connecticut, Florida, Hawaii, Indiana, Kentucky, Maine, Minnesota, Missippi, New Jersey, New Mexico, Rhode Island, Vermont, Virginia and Wisconsin.

The Illinois and Delaware statutes provide that the petition will be granted if there appears no reason for not granting it.

But even if the statute is silent on the question of reasons and purposes, the court to which the petition is presented undoubtedly, in its discretion, may refuse to grant the petition if it is satisfied that fraud or other wrong will result from the proposed change.

Such discretion, however, may not be abused. If the court acts arbitrarily, and denies the application for no good reason, an appellate court has the power to reverse the decision. The better rule (unless prohibited by statute) would appear to be that the statutory right to change one's name be co-extensive with the common law right, and put the burden on the court or the opponents to the change to show that the change is not in the public interest. (See 322 Mass. 335, 77 N.E. (2) 216) This would put an end to the too frequent pious utterances of lower court judges, and the elitism of those who cherish their names like some officers their uniforms.

The reasons which are most often advanced in support of a desired change of name relate to the difficulty in the pronunciation or spelling of the applicant's true name; the advisability confirming by court decree a name which the applicant had been using for some time previously under the right granted by the common law; the wish of a divorced mother to have her child assume the name of her subsequent husband; the belief that the new name will assist one in the practice of his trade or profession; the fact that other members of the applicant's family are using the new name, and many other reasons of convenience or utility.

The courts may look upon some reasons with sympathy and may look coldly upon others. What may satisfy the courts of one state may be obnoxious to the courts of another jurisdiction. The statutes and decisions of a particular state should be consulted by the interested person.

The consequences of an attempted change of name may sometimes be most unexpected. Where an action was brought upon an accident insurance policy the insurance company, as a defense, claimed that the application for the insurance policy contained a false representation in stating the true name of the applicant. It seems that the applicant had changed his name without court order and had used the new name for some nine years before applying for the insurance. The court held that he could recover under the policy if there was no intention to conceal his true name. (197 N.Y. 420, 90 N.E. 947) In passing, the court noted that under the New York statute, it may be that after a person has acquired a name by judicial decree, he cannot acquire a different name thereafter without resorting to the courts.

In 1946 a special election was held in New York and a legal proceeding was brought to declare invalid the candidacy of Johannes Steel, a candidate of the American Labor Party. He had come to this country in 1934, his name then being Herbert Stahl. He applied for citizenship, and at a hearing in federal court in 1938, he was asked if he wished to change his name and he said that he wished to use the name Steel instead of Stahl. There was issued to him a naturalization certificate in the name of Herbert Steel, and on the reverse it was noted that the name had been changed by court decree from Herbert Stahl. The objection to his candidacy was on the ground that since he was naturalized as Herbert Steel, he could not use the name Johannes Steel. The court rejected this contention, noting that a naturalized citizen could change his name without court proceedings. (60 N.Y.S. (2) 323) Although in New York if one changes his name by legal proceedings he may not use any other name thereafter, yet, said the court, no such prohibition exists in the federal statutes, which provide:

> "as a part of the naturalization of any person" the court may "make a decree changing the name of said person, and the certificate of naturalization shall be issued in accordance therewith." Title 8 U.S. Code Sec. 734 (e)*

Also,

> "If the name of any naturalized citizen has, subsequent to naturalization, been changed by order of any court of competent jurisdiction or by marriage, the citizen may make application for a new certificate of naturalization in the new name of such citizen."

It has been noted that in some jurisdictions it would seem that only the statutory method may be followed and that to change one's name otherwise would be unlawful. But even in the face of such statutes a court may be lenient. So, a petition for change of name was granted where the petitioner, born in Massachusetts, had used the new name in business for fifteen years and ever since his graduation from high school, and maintained a bank account in such name. Even though the statute provides the only method of change of name with legal effect, the court held that one may assume another name if done for an honest purpose, as was the rule at common law, and since the reasons for the change were consistent with public policy, it should be allowed. (320 Mass. 4, 70 N.E. (2) 249)

In Pennsylvania, a court has determined that an individual may not change his name without permission of the appropriate court, which has a wide discretion to grant or refuse the petition after hearing. If, for instance, the petitioner is a physician, lawyer or other professional person, and the change might perpetrate fraud and confusion on the public, the motive behind the change will be scrutinized closely. In the particular case, the court said that a petition of a person seeking to adopt the name of a famous personage may be denied if the change is for

* The reader is referred to How To Become A Citizen of the United States (1972), by Libby F. Jessup, one of the volumes in this series, for a thorough discussion of the subject.

"trivial or capricious or vainglorious reasons." (355 Pa. 588, 57 A. (2) 200)

If the statute requires the court to find a "sufficient reason consistent with public interest," such a finding must be made before the petition is granted. A finding to the negative must be clearly correct or an appellate court may reverse the lower court's decision.

The courts have had before them for decision a number of interesting situations where a petition for a change of name was denied. For instance, where a petition was filed in the state of California, it appeared that the petitioner had gone through bankruptcy proceedings and that as a result of such proceedings his obligations had been discharged. This, of course, was perfectly proper under the national bankruptcy act. However, when he petitioned a court to allow him to change his name, the petition was refused, the court basing its ruling on the fact that his debts had been discharged and that he had not paid them. But the petitioner was not content to abide by the lower court's decision and he appealed. The appellate court sustained the petitioner and granted his application, noting that he could change his name anyway without seeking the court's permission (i.e., by following the common law procedure), and that the granting of his petition would probably benefit his creditors by making the change of name a matter of record. (8 Cal. (2) 608, 67 P. (2) 94) The court also said:

> "If it is urged that there is some guilt or impropriety in petitioner's conduct, the obvious answer is that bankruptcy statutes were designed to relieve the debtor of his obligations and enable him to make a fresh start."

In Pennsylvania a petition to change one's name was brought under a statute of 1923. Objections were made to the petition on the ground that the petitioner had failed to furnish a certificate showing no judgments or decrees of record against him. Finally he produced a certificate which showed that there were no less than seven judgments filed against him. In addition, he had stated that he wanted to assume the name of "Marshall" which he asserted was his mother's maiden name. It turned out, however, that his mother's maiden name was "Masulla," which, said the petitioner, was translatable into English by "Marshall." The court, in view of all the facts, denied the petition and said, among other things: "It is generally known that proper names are not

subject to translation, but are spelled the same internationally."
(44 D. & C. (Pa.) 699) It may be noted that the petitioner gave
as a reason for wanting to change his name, which was Italian,
the fact that a state of war existed between the United States
and Italy and that as a consequence he was, so he said, subjected
to occasional criticism. The court said that this was not a con-
vincing reason for allowing a change of name.

Sometimes a third person will file objections to the proposed change of name on the ground that the new name is similar
to that of the objectant. Such an objection may be valid, but in
one case the court refused to deny the change of name where
the petitioner had used the name for some fourteen years before
filing the application. The court pointed out that only under
peculiar circumstances would it be justified in denying the
petition, and that the new name "constituted petitioner's legal
name, just as much as if he had borne it from birth." Further,
the court went on:

> "The purpose of the petitioner in filing this pro-
> ceeding was to establish a legal record of that which
> he had already legally done many years before. . . .
> There was no showing, however, of any fraud practiced
> upon, or of any invasion of any legal right of, remon-
> strant or any other person. . . . There was no element
> of unfair competition involved." (35 Cal. App. (2) 723,
> 96 P. (2) 958)

In the above case, which was also decided in California,
the court's opinion indicated its belief that the courts should
not discharge but should encourage petitions for change of name.

However, since judges are human, it cannot be denied
that some judges look with disfavor upon change of name proceedings, and, in the exercise of their discretionary power,
deny such applications. As we have noted, if there is reason to
believe that there has been an abuse of discretion, the petitioner
may seek relief by appealing to a higher court, provided that
such appeals are permitted in the particular jurisdiction.

It may sometimes happen that a person institutes a lawsuit
and then applies to the court for leave to have the suit proceed
under a different name. Unless such change of name is tanta-
mount to the initiation of a new or different action, or where the
statutory time limit for suits has expired, or where some fraudulent, harmful or unjust result would follow to the preduduce of

21

the defendant, the change will be allowed. (123 N.J.L. 281, 8 A. (2) 385)

An interesting situation was presented to the New Jersey courts, where a woman applied for an order to entitle her to vote in an election under the name of "Love Faith." There was no doubt that this was not the name she had been born with. However, she refused to reveal her ordinary or previous name and the election superintendent refused to allow her to vote. She thereupon prosecuted an appeal to a higher court, which decided that she would be permitted to register only if she signed her previous true name, or added such name to her registration. (22 N.J. Misc. 412, 39 A. (2) 638) The court reasoned that only thus could it be determined if she was entitled to vote, if she was a citizen, if any impersonation was involved, and if the registrant was free from any criminal convictions. A distinction was drawn between a person's "true name" and the name by which one is commonly known. In this connection, the purpose of a particular legal requirement, as contained, for example, in election laws, must be considered.

Sometimes, a court will refuse to sanction the adoption of a new name where objections are made by a family of that name, the name being very highly regarded in the community. So, in Massachusetts, a protest by a family named Cabot, sufficed to prevent the adoption of that name by a person who was entirely unrelated to them. But such cases are rare, and the courts are loath to refuse an application merely because the name is borne by another individual or family. (44 N.Y.S. (2) 2)

An interesting case in the state of New York involved an application by a person whose name was one commonly used, to change his name to one less common. In his petition, he asserted that he intended to practice the profession of podiatry, and that the change of name would assist him in his career. The court denied the application, and pointed out that honesty, character and skill were more important in a person's career than a euphonious name. The court also noted that the name borne by the petitioner was also borne by many eminent personages. (297 N.Y.S. 905)

In another case, the court had already granted permission for a change of name, and thereafter three persons, who bore the name newly taken by the petitioner, made an application to the court to vacate the order granting the application. The court denied their request, finding that no fraudulent or wrongful purpose was present. (34 N.Y.S. (2) 909) The language used by the court may interest the reader. The judge said that the original name was:

> ". . . an ancient and honorable name, but if the petitioner in the pursuit of happiness . . . desires to foresake his original name for another name, that is permissible under our system of jurisprudence. American blood is a rich mixture of many people. It has a peculiar aversion to discrimination and religious intolerance and it always sponsors a wide latitude for people in their quest for happiness. Names are relatively unimportant. In the language of Shakespeare, 'A rose by any other name would smell as sweet.' . . . Family names are not copyrighted. Every famous man has namesakes not related to him through blood or marriage and the assumed name is generally viewed as a compliment to the man whose name has been assumed."

On the other hand, to say, as have some lower courts, that the petitioner may still change his name at common law, simply by using another name consistently over a period of time without intent to deceive or avoid obligations previously incurred, even though the court will not approve his application for a judicial name change, is to skirt the issue. These cases seem to involve themselves in extra-legal sermonizing when they use their discretion to prevent speedy, judicial name changes -- Earl Green to Merwon Abdul Salaam, Robert Lee Middleton to Kikuga Nairobi Kikugus, and Russell Burleigh Douglas to Arindam -- on the bases of the proposed names' unfamiliarity, the unconventional use of a one-word name, the unproven necessity to change one's name when one adopts a new religion (Green), and the pride petitioners should have in their original American names (Green, Middleton), while suggesting the common law remedy if petitioners still want to change their names. In other words, the courts seem reluctant to grant name changes for what they deem silly or insufficient reasons. However, to deny the statutory remedy but suggest the common law remedy seems to promote even greater confusion than the confusion the court sought to eliminate by rejecting the applications. See 54 Misc. (2) 606, 283 N.Y.S. (2) 242; 60 Misc. (2) 1056, 304 N.Y.S. (2); and 60 Misc. (2) 1057, 304 N.Y.S. (2).

Of course, the mere fact that a court has denied a request for change of name in the manner provided by statute, does not preclude one from assuming any name he chooses by simply doing so under the common law rule we have mentioned earlier.

This holds, the reader will understand, subject to the qualification that the change is not made for illegal purposes.

Chapter 4

THE USE AND ABUSE OF NAMES

We have noted in the chapter dealing with the procedure for change of names that under certain circumstances a court will deny a petition for change of name if the reasons behind the proposed change are improper. We have also seen that not only will a court deny the petition, but it will do so upon the objection of a third person who has any interest in the matter, and will, upon the application of such third person, grant an order vacating a previous change of name.

But even if no formal change of name is made or requested, the use of a name may, in some cases, be prevented by a court. The situations which will give rise to such action by a court are similar to those which will induce a court to deny or vacate a formal change of name. Those reasons, as we have seen, are based upon the improper motives behind the change or use of the name.

For example, at the common law a person could prevent the use of a name by another if such use would tend to deceive the public into believing that they were dealing with the former. We see that the abuse of a name in such cases is based upon some interference with a business conducted in a man's name by a competitor who is attempting to take away such business. In other words, substantial property rights may be involved, and the courts act to protect such rights. So, in an early case in New Jersey, the court granted an injunction preventing the use of the plaintiff's picture and name in the advertising of a certain product, the court having found the existence of a property right in the name. (73 N.J. Eq. 136, 67 A. 392) Also in New Jersey, a birth certificate was ordered to be cancelled where the certificate recited that the plaintiff was the father of the child, and such recital was false. (72 N.J. Eq. 910, 67 A. 97) By giving to the child the father's name, it is clear that the latter's property rights were affected.

However, not all the states established a common law right of property in a person's name, even when associated with unauthorized use in advertising. In New York, this situation led to the enactment of a civil rights statute which provided that if a person used another person's "name, portrait or picture for advertising purposes or for purposes of trade," and such use was unauthorized, the person whose name was so used could sue for damages and obtain an injunction preventing such further use.

In an interesting New York case, a noted popular orchestra leader passed away and his widow permitted the new conductor of the orchestra to use the name of her deceased husband in connection with the orchestra billings. For this use, she was to be paid in installments, and when the new leader failed to make the payments she brought suit.

The leader claimed that the widow did now own the name of her late husband and therefore could not prevent his using it without her consent. The court said that this might be so; that under New York law, while a person could prevent the use of his name for advertising purposes without his written consent, this right would not pass to his widow after his death. However, the court went on, in this case we do not have merely an unauthorized use of the name, but a written contract with the widow, and that contract could be and would be enforced. (88 N.Y.S. (2) 225)

In Texas, a damage suit was brought because the defendant, an insurance company, made unauthorized use of the plaintiff's name in the promotion of its business. It seems that after the plaintiff had disassociated himself as manager of the company, the latter continued to use his facsimile signature on its letters. The court said that such action was improper, and that the use of the name in this fashion constituted a valuable right of property. (238 S.W. (2) (Tex.) 289)

Generally speaking, it has been said that a person has a sacred right to the honest use of his own name, and this is true even if such use may be detrimental to other persons with the same name. (242 S.W. (2) (Tex.) 777) But the right to use one's own name in a business may be transferred, and the transferror may thereafter be prevented from using his name in competition with the purchaser. And it has also been held that one could not evade his duties by creating a corporation and giving his name to the corporation.

If a person grants another permission to use his name in connection with an advertisement without any consideration for such use, it has been held that such permission may be withdrawn at any time. In a New York case involving this question (271 N.Y.S. 187), the court said:

26

"It is the well settled law of this State that a gratuitous license . . . to use name and portrait is revocable at any time, even though action has been taken upon it. The court cannot lend itself to defendant's claim that, having trade-marked the article and invested considerable money to popularize it, no revocation is possible. It may well be that by revocation serious impairment of business results. But that is a danger and risk assumed in accepting a consent unlimited as to time and against which, in the beginning, guard could easily be had. Regardless of plaintiff's reason for her refusal to continue permission to use her name, and even admitting that her reason is ulterior and mercenary, it cannot be denied that her name and her portrait are her own and during life solely at her disposal. She, therefore, cannot be gainsaid in her refusal, and defendant must be restrained."

It has been said that the New York statute on this matter, i.e., the right of privacy affecting the use of an individual's name, is a model statute on the subject. Very few states have legislation covering this branch of the law, and the judicial decisions, consequently, must be examined with care.

Chapter 5

FICTITIOUS AND ASSUMED NAMES

We are all familiar with the fact that many persons, occupying the highest stations in life, authors, artists, scientists, and other eminent personalities, have found it expedient or advisable to adopt other names in connection with their vocations. Voltaire, the great French philosopher and writer, was born Francois Marie Arouet; the ancestral name of de Balzac was Balssa, and the "de" was added by Balzac himself; the Dutch scholar Desiderius Erasmus was borth with the name Gerhard Gerhards or Geerts; and the French playwright Jean Baptiste Poquelin took the pseudonym Molière. And in our own country, the famous humorists Samuel L. Clemens and Charles R. Browne respectively took unto themselves the pen names Mark Twain and Artemus Ward. On the other hand, some writers have been so identified with their fictional creations that their own names have suffered. Finley Peter Dunne and Arthur Train were better known as "Mr. Dooley" and "Mr. Tutt" than by their true names. The reader undoubtedly can extend the list to many pages.

So there is nothing improper in the assumption of a fictitious name or a "nom de plume," if the purpose behind the change is honest. And it may be noted that even if another person bears the same name, that of itself is no reason to bar the taking of the name. We have discussed some phases of this question in our chapter on the motives behind the change of name.

There are occasions when a court must decide whether there was in the situation before it a genuine assumption of a new name. In the federal court in Ohio a man brought a suit to recover on a fire insurance policy which covered certain real estate that had been damaged by fire. The events which preceded the fire were curious. It seems that the plaintiff had acquired the property some twenty years earlier. Thereafter, he had become involved in an accident in which a person had been injured and, apparently fearing a judgment against him, had made a deed of the property which purported to convey the property to a person we will call Mrs. E. S. Not long after another deed was made which purported to transfer the property from Mrs. E. S. to a Mrs. E. M. Then another deed was prepared from Mrs. E. M. to one C. K., and finally a deed was made conveying the property back to the original owner, the plaintiff. All the deeds had been prepared by the plaintiff or his wife, and no such persons as E. S., E. M., or C. K. existed. The insurance company, however, claimed that Mrs. E. S. and Mrs. E. M. were really other names assumed by the plaintiff's wife, that the deed to C. K. was invalid because there was no such person and, therefore, that C. K. could not make a deed to the plaintiff. Accordingly, argued the insurance company, the plaintiff did not own the property when the fire occurred.

But, said the court, all the names were fictitious and all the intermediate deeds were void so that the plaintiff was always the owner of the property, and since the plaintiff's wife had never used the other names it could not be said that she had assumed them as her own. Therefore she at no time was a legal owner of the property. (135 F. (2) 479)

This case was complicated, and it is typical of the way in which courts will look to the realities of a situation and not be led astray by superficial factors.

In another case, a person sought to escape military service in a European country and took the name of his brother, who was alive. He also used the same name in applying for a visa to this country. After he arrived here, he resumed his true name. When he subsequently applied for naturalization, his application was denied because of the fact that he had assumed another name when he came here. He appealed to the courts and his petition was granted. The court said that in fact the name he had when he entered the country (his brother's name) was at the time his real name; that the name was as legal as though given to him at birth. The fact that he took the name of another living person does not change the rule, and after arriving here he had the right to assume his own name again (49 F. Sup 953)

The question has arisen whether the use of an assumed or fictitious name may constitute the crime of forgery. A conviction for forgery was sustained where the defendant had issued a check on a bank in which he had no account and used an assumed name which apparently had been made up on the spur of the moment. It was important to determine the meaning of the word "forgery," and the court considered two possible definitions. A "narrow" construction defines forgery as "the making or altering of a document with intent to defraud or prejudice another so as to make it appear to be a document made by another." A broader construction defines forgery as "the false making of an instrument, which purports on the face of it to be good and valid for the purposes for which it was created, with a design to defraud any person or persons." The narrow definition contemplates a fraudulent use by one person of the name of another adopted person; the broad definition seems to contemplate the use of an assumed name used for a dishonest purpose. The court adtopted the broad definition. (38 Wash. (2) 475, 230 P. (2) 786)

It may even be possible to commit forgery by using one's own name when it is identical with the name of another person, and the document is passed off as that of the other person.

Whether the assumption of the new name is done under the common law rule which permits a change of name without court sanction, or whether the change is accomplished formally pursuant to the statutes providing therefor, the change is equally valid. This of course presumes that there is no positive prohibition against the change in the particular jurisdiction and that the change is otherwise proper.

In a related situation, the defendant in a criminal trial may attempt to prove that his identity has not been sufficiently established. In one case, the court held that there is a "presumption of identity of person from identity of name." (121 Cal. App. (2) 17, 262 P. (2) 630)

But the use of fictitious names has not been the sole prerogative of individuals. Countless numbers of business enterprises, conducted by partnerships or by individuals are being carried on under assumed names. And we are all familiar with the artificial names of corporations.

CONDUCTING BUSINESS UNDER AN ASSUMED NAME

In the absense of a controlling statute, there is no legal reason why a person may not undertake to carry on a business under an assumed name. But the majority of states do, in fact, have statutes which regulate such activity. Therefore, the individual who plans to conduct a business under a fictitious name should check the laws of his own state or, still better, consult an attorney, in order to determine if his state has enacted a fictitious names act or assumed names act, as such statutes are often called.

The consequences of failing to register an assumed name where such registration is required may be very serious. Failure to comply with the statute is usually made a misdemeanor, subject to fine or imprisonment or both. And in some states, a person who has failed to register his business name may find that he cannot bring suit to recover an obligation owed to the concern.

One must be familiar with not only the applicable laws as to fictitious or assumed names, but also the applicable provisions of the uniform commercial code of that state. Although not readily available to the layman, a set called American Jurisprudence Pleading and Practice Forms (Vol. 18, "Name" Part II) carries a list of applicable state statutes.

In Pennsylvania an action was brought to recover the amount of a check which had been issued by the defendant and upon which payment had been stopped. One of the defenses asserted by the maker of the check was that the plaintiff had failed to register his business name under the state's fictitious name act, and therefore could not sue. The statute, which was enacted in 1945, specifically said that no action could be brought on any contract until the act was complied with. The court, accordingly, was compelled to dismiss the plaintiff's case, but did so without prejudice to the plaintiff's right to start a new suit after registering the name. (68 D. & C. (Pa.) 406)

The importance of the exact wording of the statute is seen in a case in Pennsylvania which was brought to compel the defendant to stop using the name "New Motor Court." The case was dismissed, because the court held that the operator of a business establishment could not exclusively appropriate the single word "new" as a portion of his name. But for our purposes it is important to see what the court said when, as one defense, the defendant claimed the plaintiff could not sue because it had failed to register its name. In this respect, said the court, the defendant was wrong, because, under the statute as it existed in Pennsylvanis in 1942, the failure to file a certificate did not bar the right to equitable relief, assuming that other grounds for such relief existed. (45 D. & C. (Pa.) 432)

In Illinois a broker was not precluded from suing and recovering his brokerage commission merely because he had failed to comply with the assumed name act of that state. (343 Ill. App. 515, 99 N. E. (2) 567)

On the other hand, where an estate was administered under the married name of the deceased who went under a professional name in her business, it was held that creditors could bring an action against the estate despite the fact that administration of the estate had been completed. It was incumbent upon the administrators to include the professional as well as the married name of the deceased so that notice would be proper, as is essential in the administration of estates. (487 P. (2) 925 (1971)

In Illinois a court has decided that the failure to file a registration certificate would not preclude the plaintiff from bringing an action for breach of contract, that the failure to register was a criminal offense, and that each day of failure to register was a separate offense and violation of the act. (408 Ill. 61, 96 N. E. (2) 97) The court quoted from another case, the language of which may be of interest:

> "The remedial purpose of the statute manifestly was that the public should have ready means of information as to the personal or financial responsibility behind the assumed name. Its aim was the protection of those who might deal with or give credit to the fictitious entity. It obviously was not to provide a means by which persons having received a benefit from another should be enabled to retain it without compensation and to repudiate any agreement for compensation. Doubtless a penalty which held out a reasonable promise of securing compliance with the statute was intended; but one which had in it the possibility of a year's imprisonment would seem to be adequate to accomplish that end, and it would seem that a further penalty such as the defendants contend for would create a cumulative penal result with which the evil sought to be remedied was scarcely commensurate." (89 Conn. 293, 93 A. 1027)

The language of the court above quoted is an excellent summary of the purpose behind the registration laws. Most of the states permit a plaintiff to sue even if he has failed to register an assumed business name. In any case, the person conducting business under an assumed name should ascertain whether in his state the statutory penalties are exclusive or whether failure to comply with the statute will also prevent him from applying to the courts for the protection of his rights of property.

At this point, the reader is reminded of the situation presented earlier where we saw that a false statement in a petition for change of name relating to the filing of a business certificate influenced the court to deny the petition.

We have said that the registration of an assumed name for business purposes is required in practically every state. But some jurisdictions appear to have no statutory control in the matter, including the District of Columbia, Kansas, Mississippi, New Mexico, South Dakota, Tennessee, Wisconsin and Wyoming. In the states of Nebraska and South Carolina it seems that only partnership certificates must be filed, showing the identities of the partners, but there seems to be no requirement for the recording of trade names otherwise. ·

The question of the proper or improper registration of trade names is sometimes brought before the federal courts, and in such cases the courts apply the rule of law of the particular state in which the federal court is situated. The jurisdiction of the federal courts depends, among other things, on the fact that the parties are citizens of different states. Where an action was brought in a federal court to restrain the defendant from using a business name in connection with the sale of beer, it appeared that the plaintiff had the same family name as that given to the product. But since no unfair competition was involved the court denied the plaintiff's request for an injunction, saying that the plaintiff had no property right to be protected from anyone who wanted to use his family name in the absence of any injury actually suffered by the plaintiff. (37 F. Sup. 79)

Where the plaintiff in a lawsuit alleged in his complaint that he and another person were conducting business under an assumed name, but in fact the registration certificate which had been filed indicated that only the plaintiff was registered as doing business under the fictitious name, the court held that the facts did not warrant a dismissal of the complaint. (13 F. (2) 68)

See Chapter Eight for a further discussion of business names.

Chapter 6

YOUR NAME AND YOUR IDENTITY

The primary function of a name is to identify an individual, to set him or her apart from all other individuals, so far as that may be accomplished. Evidently, unless each person born in the world is assigned a unique symbol, such as a number, the method of identification by use of a name is not foolproof. Because of the similarity of names possessed by several individuals, the courts are, therefore, frequently called upon to determine questions of identity, particularly in connection with legal documents. In this chapter we will touch upon some of the problems faced by the courts and the ways in which they attempt to dispose of them.

LEGAL DOCUMENTS

In an action to recover possession of certain real property in the state of Mississippi, it appears that a deed had been signed with the initial "B." followed by the signer's surname. Thereafter a mortgage sale of the property was held, and the notice of the sale stated that it would be sold by "B. B.," followed by the same surname. The reader will note that an additional "B." appears in the notice of sale which thus differed from the deed. The court decided that the notice was fatally defective, and the plaintiff consequently lost his case. In its opinion the court noted that a person's name ordinarily consists of one or more Christian or given names and one surname or family name, and the the use of initials or first letters of the Christian name is permissible in designating a person. However, the court held the notice of sale to be defective, not because of the use of initials, but because of the insertion of the additional "B.," thus making it appear that another person was intended. (183 Miss. 151, 183 So. 920)

In another lawsuit involving a deed, this time in the state of Montana, the court recognized the identity of a person whose first name was given as "Saml." in a deed to him, and as "Samuel" in a deed from him to another. The court pointed out that it is sufficient to describe a person by any known and accepted abbreviation of his Christian name, and that there are certain standard abbreviations, derivatives and nicknames for the more common Christian names which have long been recognized by the courts as being interchangeable with the person's full name. (124 Mont. 463, 226 P. (2) 487) Among such abbreviations are the well known Alex for Alexander, Bill or Wm. for William, Bob for Robert, Dan for Daniel, Geo. for George, Jon. or Jack for John, etc. Where such abbreviations are used, it is probable that a court would hold as in the above case, to wit, that the abbreviation may be used interchangeably with the full name.

But wherever possible a person should endeavor to achieve a correspondence of names and a correct expression of his identity. It is evident that when a name is used in a legal document it must correctly identify the person to whom it relates. To identify a person in a document of legal importance, such as a will or deed, by a name other than that by which he is commonly known, may result in grave injustice which may require extended litigation to correct. And sometimes correction may not be possible.

As a general principle of law, a person's middle name or initial is not considered of great consequence legally. This question has been brought before the courts on numerous occasions.

In an Illinois case, one of the issues was whether a person whom we will call "John Doe" was the same as "John B. Doe." Upon the facts in the particular case, the court found that such identity was not shown. The court noted that a real question of identity was involved, and therefore the general rule that the middle initial is not part of the name did not apply, and that the middle initial or any other characteristic about the name in question may be of great importance to establish identity. (282 Ill. App. 52)

In Alabama, an action was brought against a defendant who was referred to in the complaint as "J. R. Oden," when in fact it was intended that one "J. W. Oden" be made the defendant. When the case came to trial, "J. W." appeared and defended the action, apparently recognizing that he was the true defendant. Under the circumstances, therefore, the court allowed the plaintiff to amend the complaint to show the correct middle initial. In the course of its opinion, the court said: "The change involved in this amendment was that of the middle initial, which under our decisions is accorded little notice. * * * the law takes no notice of the middle initial." (235 Ala. 363, 179 So. 191)

But, as has been noted above, the courts may take notice of the middle initial or any other circumstance if a real question of identity presents itself for determination.

An interesting lawsuit was brought in Indiana to compel the election commissioners to place the plaintiff's name on a ballot as a candidate for public office. In his declaration of candidacy he used the name "Gene G." followed by his surname. However, as a voter he had used the first names "Eugene Gabriel." Here, of course, no real question of identity was involved. The court took judicial notice of the usual corruptions and abbreviations of Christian names in common use, and found that "Gene" and "Eugene" could be regarded as synonymous. Ordinarily, went on the court, the law recognized only one given name, and the middle name or the initial thereof could be rejected as surplusage. The court, therefore, decided the issue in favor of the plaintiff. (217 Ind. 179, 26 N. E. (2) 1002)

The question of identity often plagues the courts in criminal as well as in civil actions, and frequently arises in connection with the construction of indictments.

In Georgia an indictment for robbery set forth the first name of the person robbed as "James" and later on referred to him as "Jim." Based upon this discrepancy, the defendant moved (that is, requested the court) to dismiss the indictment. But the court upheld the validity of the indictment, saying: "The ordinary significance of 'James' and 'Jim' is that Jim is but an abbreviation for James so far as proper names are concerned. . . . The names are synonymous. . . . it was proper for the court to permit testimony for the purpose of showing" that the names referred to "one and the same person." (72 Ga. App. 11, 32 S. E. (2) 848)

A resident of the state of Pennsylvania made a will in which he bequeathed certain property to the "Penna. S.P.C.A." The court took judicial notice that the meaning of the abbreviation was the Pennsylvania Society for the Prevention of Cruelty to Animals and allowed the bequest to stand. The test to be applied, said the court, is whether the abbreviation used in the will is of such general and public notoriety that every reasonably informed person may fairly be presumed to be acquainted with it. (346 Pa. 610, 31 A. (2) 280)

However, the reader will be well advised to avoid the use of abbreviations wherever the full name may be used instead.

In a New York case, the testator made a will which was in the form of a letter addressed to "My dear Joe!" The court held that the beneficiary was sufficiently identified when it appeared, by evidence taken in court, who "Dear Joe" was. (132 N.Y.S. 257) And in an early English case, a legacy to a person referred to in the will only as a "Mrs. G." was allowed to stand where the identity of the person so denominated was established to the court's satisfaction.

Another English case even held that a legacy may be given to a certain person when there is no such person in existence as was described in the will, as "to John A. Style," where there was no such person, but the testator used to call a certain person by that name. In other words, a person who may be known to the testator as "A.B.," and to all other persons as "C.D.," may take a legacy given to "A.B." (78 N.H. 224, 99 A. 18)

The principle is that if a person is commonly known by a name which is not properly his and which may, in fact, even belong to another person, it nevertheless may be said that the name, even though false in its application, describes the former person. Evidence might have to be introduced to show which person was intended. Nicknames may sometimes be used, and are no less a description of the person to whom they are applied, although not as correct.

From what has been said, it will appear that while identity of name is some proof of identity of person, it is not conclusive identification, and all surrounding circumstances will be considered. (140 F. (2) 83) A legacy given to a person who is identified by a nickname will be upheld if it can be shown that he was so known to the testator. It is the facts and circumstances to which the courts look in such cases, and even a mistake in the name or description of a legatee in a will will not necessarily render the legacy void if the person intended can be identified from all others.

It has been said that extrinsic evidence may be used to show that an apparent uncertainty on the face of a document does not really exist. (175 Ky. 80, 193 S. W. 1013) It is the individual's identity that is material and not the name, the name being only one of many ways in which identity may be determined. Apart from the person's identity, it may be said that the name itself is of minor importance.

Persons may be improperly named in legal proceedings or lawsuits, but the courts will not necessarily dismiss a suit for that reason alone. (10 F. 894) A person may even be designated in a legal action by a name which is not his true name, if he is commonly known thereby, and it has been held that the pleadings in a lawsuit are not insufficient merely because the initials of the parties instead of their full Christian names were used. (283 F. 552) In one case a person was served with a subpoena to testify in an action, the subpoena giving the name of the witness as (we shall say) "John W. Doe," whereas his true name was "John R. Doe." He actually did appear in court and testified, and the court said that it could not be urged that "John W. Doe" named in the subpoena did not testify, or that another witness had been produced. (23 F. (2) 977)

In Oklahoma, a bank had obtained a judgment against a person named Ryan. Thereafter the bank, now a judgment-creditor, brought another suit against the same defendant on the judgment in the state of Texas. Among other defenses, the defendant contended that it was not shown that the defendant in the Oklahoma judgment and the defendant in Texas was the same person. The court said:

> "A person with the same name as the defendant in the Oklahoma judgment filed an answer in the Texas case that shows said parties are identical. Furthermore, 'the identity of the person sued with the one against whom the judgment was recovered may be presumed if the names given in full are the same.' "(186 S. W. (2) 747)

In Missouri, under a habitual criminal statute, the defendant was convicted of perjury and his sentence was, accordingly, more severe. Prior records of conviction were introduced and the defendant complained that the records did not establish his identity with the person previously convicted. Aside from evidence of similarity in height, color of hair and color of eyes, the court said that mere identity of names is prima facie sufficient evidence of identity of person. (354 Mo. 337, 189 S. W. (2) 314)

MIDDLE NAMES AND INITIALS

Aside from the instances noted above in this chapter, the importance of first names, middle names and initials has been considered by the courts in other connections.

The importance attached to the first name may be seen in the following few cases.

A tax assessment in Illinois was made against a property owner whose name was Wilmer Hiram Dunn. However, in the tax assessment roll the property owner's name was listed as Hiram Dunn. The matter was litigated, and in court the owner testified that he had never been known as or called by the name of Hiram. The court, accordingly, dismissed a judgment for taxes against him holding that he had never been a proper party to the tax proceeding and that the court had never acquired jurisdiction over him. The court said that the law recognizes only one Christian name, and a middle name or initial is not material in any legal proceeding. (247 Ill. 410, 93 N. E. 305)

In another similar case in Missouri, a tax judgment was obtained and property was sold to satisfy the judgment. The judgment had been obtained after service of the summons had been made by publication against the defendant, who was a nonresident of the state, his name being given in the summons as Owen Corrigan. His real name was John Owen Corrigan. The court pointed out that where service of a summons is made by publication, the forms of the law must be more strictly observed than where service is made by delivering the summons to the defendant personally. Therefore, said the court, there was a fatal misnomer in the summons and the judgment was void. (126 Mo. 304, 28 S. W. 874)

In a New Jersey action one of the questions which the court had to determine was whether a judgment obtained against a person called in the judgment "Edward Morris" ("Edward" being the middle and not the Christian name of the judgment debtor) was valid as against a person who had acquired certain real estate from Morris. It seems that in the transfer of the property Morris had been referred to as T. Edward Morris or as Thomas E. Morris. There was no question that "Edward," 'T. Edward" and "Thomas E." were the same person, but the serious issue was whether an innocent purchaser of the property was protected from the judgment. The court said that he was not bound by the judgment and took the property free and clear of any judgment lien. The point is that the judgment was docketed against Edward Morris and a person buying from "T. Edward or "Thomas E." Morris could not be expected to know that "T. Edward" as the same person. (85 N. J. Eq. 476, 97 A. 42)

But the importance of the middle name or middle initial

is also shown in some situations, where the circumstances require that the middle name or initial be taken into consideration.

In Alabama, one "J. A." Johnson executed a chattel mortgage on certain personal property in favor of the plaintiff. Several months later a similar mortgage on the same property was executed by "J. F." Johnson in favor of the defendant. If, said the court, the initials "J. A." were the true initials of the mortgagor, then the plaintiff would prevail in the lawsuit, but if the true initials were "J. F.," then the defendant's rights were not affected by the previous mortgage. This was a question for the jury to determine. (197 Ala. 427, 73 S. 72) So we see that a mistake in the middle initial of a recorded mortgage may possibly prevent constructive notice to a subsequent buyer or mortgagee of the property.

Involving again the validity of the service of a summons by publication on and a judgment against one "A. L." (followed by surname) was a case in Colorado. The property had thereafter been conveyed to the plaintiff by "A. S." (followed by surname), and the question was whether the plaintiff's title to the property was affected by the prior judgment. The court held that the plaintiff's title was not affected by the judgment, because the variance in the names was too great under the circumstances, despite the general rule that the law does not regard a middle name or initial as essential in designating a person. (135 P. (Colo.) 121) The court said:

> "The middle name or initial in a person's name has become quite material in modern times, especially as a distinguishing identification of a person. Many persons now have the same Christian, or given, name, and the same patronymic, family, or surname, and it is by the middle name or initial, only, in many instances, that the person may be distinguished or identified in writing."

In another proceeding, the question was whether certain real estate tracts in the names of "W. N. Morris" and "W. U. Morris" respectively were the same, and whether the record of a deed in the former name would constitute due notice of a claim to property which was recorded in the latter name. The court said that the issue was not one of idem sonans (same sound), (as to which see p. 42), but one of identity, and that

"W. N. Morris" and "W. U. Morris" are not identical names of the same persons. (18 Tex. Civ. App. 472, 44 S. W. 1073)

DEFAMATION*

In order to determine if a statement is defamatory, that is, whether or not it attacks a person's character and is legally actionable, one of the things which must be ascertained, of course, is whether the statement refers to a specific person. In other words, when a plaintiff brings an action for damages based upon libel or slander, he must show, among other things, that the statement identifies him.

It may be that a person is improperly named but should it clearly be demonstrated that the defamatory utterance is directed at him, then he may maintain a legal action.

Sometimes a person is unintentionally libeled, as where a newspaper article attacks a person by name, believing that such person is entirely fictitious. But should there actually be a person of that name, the newspaper may be liable in a defamation action. In an English case,** the court said, in this connection:

> ". . . if, in the opinion of a jury, a substantial number of persons who knew the plaintiff, reading the article, would believe that it refers to him, in my opinion an action, assuming the language to be defamatory, can be maintained; and it makes no difference whether the writer inserted the name or description unintentionally, by accident, or believing that no person existed corresponding with the name or answering the description. If upon the evidence the jury are of the opinion that ordinary sensible readers, knowing the plaintiff, would be of opinion that the article referred to him, the plaintiff's case is made out."

* The reader is referred to The Law of Libel and Slander (1973), by Ella C. Thomas, one of the volumes in this series, for a thorough discussion of the subject.

** 2 K.B. 444, Aff'd. (1910) A.C. 20, 16 Ann. Cas. 166.

IDEM SONANS

The courts sometimes seek the assistance of another legal principle to assist them in solving questions of identity which turn on the similarity of names. The principle is known to lawyers as idem sonans, which in Latin means literally "same sound." The reader will perceive that this rule is applied to names which may differ in their spelling and which may yet be exactly the same or substantially the same in sound.

For the purposes of this principle, a name which sounds exactly or substantially the same as another will generally be considered to be the same, despite what may be a considerable variance in the way the two names are spelled. This idem sonans rule is really an additional evidential fact which is used to determine a person's identity, particularly as used in legal proceedings and in legal documents.

In a federal criminal proceeding, a man was indicted as "W. J. Faust." In fact, his true name was "W. J. Foust." It will be seen that the two names sound practically the same. The defendant applied to the court to dismiss the indictment, claiming that there was a material variance between the name as used in the indictment and his true name. The court invoked the idem sonans rule and denied the defendant's request, holding that the difference in spelling did not constitute a material variance. (163 U.S. 452)

The reader may be interested in a few examples in which the courts have made use of the rule and in which they have refused to do so. The courts have held that the following names were not idem sonans: Tanssing, Livingston & Co. and Taussig, Livingstone & Co.; Spintz and Sprinz; Jeffery and Jeffries; Chester and Chesley; Ferrel and Ferril; Stouse and Stout; McMurry and McMurrain. The following names have been held to be idem sonans: Whitman and Witman; Seymore and Seymour; Rauch and Rouch; Hankins and Hankines; Lindsay and Lindsey.

In all cases involving the application of the rule the guiding principle is whether a listener would find any difficulty in making a distinction between the names upon hearing them pronounced. Of course, no court will invoke the idem sonans rule if to do so would prejudice a person unfairly or would work any other injustice.

In a prosecution in the state of Georgia, the written accusation, in several places, made reference to the defendant as John "Thomson" instead of his true name which was

"Thompson." The court applied the _idem sonans_ rule and quoted from a leading text on criminal law in the following language:

> "Idem sonans means of the same sound. . . . the rule in idem sonans is, that the variance is immaterial unless it is such as misleads the party to his prejudice." (58 Ga. App. 679, 199 S. E. 787)

In another prosecution, this time for bigamy in the state of South Carolina, the indictment stated that the defendant had been previously married to a person named "Hutchinson" whereas in fact it appeared that she had married a man named "Harrington." The appellate court decided that the indictment was fatally defective and that the rule of _idem sonans_ could not be applied in this case. The name of the person to whom the defendant was allegedly married was most material and there was not sufficient similarity between the two names which would justify the court in holding that they came within the rule. (197 S. C. 154, 14 S. E. (2) 898)

A North Carolina indictment gave the defendant's name as "Vincent." This seems to have been erroneous, since the name he frequently used was in fact "Vinson" and, furthermore, the defendant alleged that his "true" name was "Furgurson." In upholding the conviction, the court said:

> "Whatever the defendant's real name may be, there can be no doubt that the person who was tried under the name of . . . Vincent pleaded to the indictment under this name and was identified by the prosecutrix as her assailant. He was sentenced under the name of . . . Vincent, and he is now held in custody under the same name. It seems to be a clear case of idem sonans, there being no question as to the identity of the defendant. . . . the defendant will not now be heard to say his real name is 'Fergurson'. He was tried under the name of Vincent, without objection or challenge, and sentenced under the same name. There being no questions as to his identity, he may retain the name for purposes of judgment." (222 N. C. 543, 23 S. E. (2) 832)

The _idem sonans_ principle has been applied by the courts in civil as well as in criminal proceedings, as the following examples will demonstrate.

In Ohio a suit was brought for the specific performance of a contract for the purchase of real estate, that is, to compel the defendant to take the property and pay the purchase price. The defendants claimed by way of defense that the plaintiff had failed to show that his title to the property was "marketable" or "merchantable" as he had agreed. Among other things the court was called on to decide if the names "Esterly" and "Easterly," which appeared in the record, or "chain" of title, were sufficiently alike to make applicable the principle of idem sonans. The court answered this question in the affirmative, and held that the marketability of the title was not affected by the difference in the spelling of the names. However, the court said that, for other reasons, the title was not marketable and dismissed plaintiff's petition. (72 Oh. App. 187, 51 N. E. (2) 41)

A similar situation was presented in a South Dakota legal proceeding to have title to real property declared merchantable, since a purchaser could not be compelled to accept a conveyance of the property if the state of the title was reasonably doubtful. It appeared that the record chain of title showed "John B. Peterson and Kate Peterson" as mortgagors, while in later foreclosure proceedings their names were given as "Petersen." The court said that this did not affect the title and quoted from a text on the subject of titles as follows:

"There is a presumption that differently spelled names refer to the same person, when they sound alike, or when the attentive ear finds difficulty in distinguishing them, or when common usage has by corruption or abbreviation made their pronounciation identical, e.g., Conolly and Conley, Macomber and McComber." (70 S. D. 562, 21 N. W. (2) 213)

Chapter 7

THE MARRIED WOMAN AND HER NAME

(Note: This chapter was written for publication in 1954. Substantial changes have been made in the law since that time. Additions to the original author's writing will be enclosed in brackets.)

We will discuss in this chapter the rights of a married woman with respect to her name, that is, with respect to the use of her maiden name and the surname of her husband. In Chapter two we have already mentioned some of the legal problems arising when a woman who is divorced wishes to resume her maiden name or the name of a prior husband, but here we will consider some legal aspects of the wife's name during the marriage state. Before going into the subject of names proper, however, we will review the general status of a married woman, both under the old common law conceptions and under the modern statutes.

In England, from which we derive many of our legal principles, the old common law merged the personality of the wife with that of her husband. So far as the law was concerned, it was, except in some special circumstances, as if the wife lost her existence when she entered into a marriage. However, over a period of many centuries, her legal disabilities, both with respect to her husband and with respect to third persons, were removed, and today a married woman, under the so-called Married Women's Acts, may enter into all types of contracts, as well with her husband as with others, and may even sue her husband as if he were a stranger. In some states this process of emancipation has gone farther than in others, but almost everywhere she is considered a separate entity from her husband, although, of course, the husband is still liable for her support and is the legal head of the family. Except in some unusual situations, as where the husband abandons his wife, his domicile is considered to be hers also.

This theoretical identity of the wife with her husband at the early common law was expressed by the famous common law jurist, Blackstone, as follows:

> "By marriage the husband and wife are one person in law; that is the very being or legal existence of the woman is suspended during the marriage, or at least is incorporated and consolidated into that of the husband; under whose wing, protection, and cover, she performs everything; and is therefore called in our law-French, a feme-covert, * * *; is said to be a covert-baron, or under the protection and influence of her husband, her baron, or lord; and her condition during her marriage is called her coverture. Upon this principle, of a union of person in husband and wife, depend almost all the legal rights, duties, and disabilities, that either of them acquire by the marriage. I speak not at present of the rights of property, but of such as are merely personal. For this reason, a man cannot grant anything to his wife, or enter into covenant with her: for the grant would be to suppose her separate existence; and to covenant with her, would be only to covenant with himself; and therefore it is also generally true, that all compacts made between husband and wife, when single, are voided by the intermarriage." Commentaries, 442.

Such was the condition of the wife at common law, and the reader will see to what extent the status of the married woman has changed at the present time. However, what may appear absurd to us, living in the twentieth century, was by no means absurd when considered in the light of the economic and social conditions prevailing in an earlier time.

Today all is changed; the property relations between the spouses are entirely different, the wife being a distant legal entity, having the right to dispose of her property as she wills, and enter into other economic relations, and the husband's control over her person (at the old common law a husband could physically chastise his wife) and property is practically nonexistent.

But in the matter of the married woman's name, the old tradition persists; the wife still bears her husband's name.

In an early case in the state of South Carolina (68 S.C. 535), a wife, in the course of a matrimonial action, requested the court to be allowed to change her name from that of her husband to that of her first husband. The court denied the petition and said:

> "The Court undoubtedly possesses the power to change the name of a party who may make such an application for such person. If in this mode the name of the husband was changed, that of the wife would also be changed, as a necessary consequence. But an application to change the name of a wife without the concurrence and consent of the husband is without precedent. It seems also to be wrong in principle. How do I know that these parties may not become reconciled? Reunions more improbable have occurred. It would be wrong in the Court to throw any impediment in the way of such reconciliation in addition to those that already so unhappily exist."

While a court may be reluctant to change the name of a married woman to a name other than that of her husband, there seems to be no legal bar to her assuming her maiden or any other name without the permission of a court. We see such changes constantly in the entertainment and commercial worlds, where women pursue their careers under their maiden or assumed names.

In 1931 an inquiry was made of the then Attorney General of the State of New York relating to the issuance of a license to a married woman in her maiden name, and the attorney general replied in a letter which the reader may find of interest. The letter is dated November 24, 1931, and reads as follows:

> "Your letter of November 18th inquires if it is the custom of the law that a woman must take her husband's name after marriage, and if you have the right to issue an undertaker's license to such woman under her maiden name. You state that the application for this license is made in the woman's maiden name; that in her personal interview before your Committee on Character and Fitness she testified to the fact that she is married, but uses her maiden name for business reasons and

47

has an agreement with her husband and with the church to do this.

"It also appears from the transcript of her testimony before your Committee that she never uses her married name at any time in her business and that her father has carried on a similar business before her marriage, and that it is claimed that the family name is well known in business dealings. The applicant also states in her testimony that she has always used her family name and intends to continue to do so. It is my opinion that this woman may continue to use her maiden name and that you may lawfully issue an undertaker's license to her in her maiden name.

"It is customary, of course, for the wife to adopt the name of her husband, and a person has the right to adopt any name that he may desire and use it as his own, unless a person does so in order to defraud others through mistake of identity. It is the identity of the individual that is regarded and not the name that he may bear or assume. The woman in the present case does not lose her identity or rights by marriage, and if she desires to use her maiden name, I can see no harm in it as long as she does not use it to defraud others."

An interesting case which dealt with the right of a married woman to prevent another woman from using the name of the former's husband arose in the state of New York and was decided in 1929 in favor of the latter. In that case the plaintiff wife brought an action against her husband and against another woman in which the plaintiff asked the court to adjudge that she was the lawful wife of the man defendant; that the defendants were not husband and wife; that an alleged divorce obtained by the defendant husband from the plaintiff was void and that an alleged remarriage with the defendant woman was also void. The court decided in favor of the plaintiff on these issues, but the court further held that it would not issue an injunction to restrain the woman defendant from assuming or using the husband's surname. (250 N.Y. 382, 165 N.E. 819)

The court noted that upon marriage a woman takes her husband's name and that the plaintiff had a legal right to the use of such name. However, said the court, the plaintiff does not have an exclusive right to the use of the name; there is no claim that the defendant woman was impersonating the plaintiff or that the plaintiff would be injured because of a mistake in identity. The only injury, said the court, was an injury to the plaintiff's feelings, and for such an injury an injunction would not be granted.

In Illinois a man filed a complaint to declare his alleged marriage with the defendant to be null and void on the ground that he was kidnapped, threatened with a gun and an attempt made by the defendant and others to force him to marry the defendant. Among other things, there arose the question whether the court could order the defendant not to use the plaintiff's name or any abbreviation thereof. The court decided that such an order would be improper, saying:

> ". . . it may be noted that by the Statute . . . that anyone after residing in this State for six months may assume any name he or she desires, by appearing by petition in the court in compliance with such statute and, by consent of court and proper finding in a decree, have his or her name changed or a new one adopted in lieu of his or her former name. The injunctional order as issued in the instant case would tend to interfere with such a proceeding and the operation of said statute." (298 Ill. App. 510, 19 N.E. (2) 137)

The incorrect or improper use of a married woman's name can sometimes lead to most interesting situations, whether such use is made by the married woman herself or by other persons who are dealing with her.

In one case in Alabama, the physicians who treated a deceased woman before her death filed a claim for medical services and the claim was made in the name of "Mrs. J. C. Jones." The decedent's name was "Hattie W. Jones" and it was proven that "Mrs. J. C. Jones" and "Hattie W. Jones" were in fact the same person. Accordingly, the court allowed the claim, saying:

> "Admittedly, in a strict sense, decedent's name was not Mrs. J. C. Jones, as a married woman takes her husband's surname with which is used her own given name: or, to state it differently, a married woman's name consists, in law, of her own Christian name and her husband's surname." (233 Ala. 658, 133 So. 38)

The court then quoted from a Nebraska case to the effect

that by a social custom which so largely prevails that it may be called a general one, the wife is designated by the Christian name or names of her husband, or the initial letter or letters of such Christian name or names, together with the abbreviation "Mrs." prefixed to the surname, and all married women, with few exceptions, are better known by such name than their own Christian name, used with their husband's surname, and that their identification would be more perfect and complete by the use of the former method than the latter. The main object to be accomplished, as we have noted earlier in this book in the chapter on identity, is to establish the identity of the person involved.

[Nebraska has since affirmed this decision (164 Neb. 593, 83 N.W. (2) 51), relying on its own precedents and those of legal encyclopedias. This may be the place to sermonize against the use of encyclopedias of law to establish or support a precedent. Legal encyclopedias are case finders and their editors are not paid to do any more than state the law. Law, inevitably, is guilty of cultural lag; and encyclopedias, reflecting the law, lag even further behind. In the appendices to this book the reader will find cases and articles that probe much deeper into the origin of surnames and offer a more balanced and less chauvinistic view of a woman's right to a name of her choice.]

In Massachusetts an unusual case presented the following features: The plaintiff, a passenger in a taxicab, was injured in a collision between the taxicab and an automobile owned by the defendant, a married woman, which was driven by the latter's son, without her authority. The court found that the son was not negligent, that is, he was not to blame for the accident, but the plaintiff tried to hold the defendant liable anyway. The plaintiff's theory was that the defendant's car was registered in the name of "Mrs. John P. Williams" and that is should have been registered in the name of "Ethel M. Williams"; that the car was, therefore, unlawfully on the highway, and for that reason the defendant was liable. The court denied the plaintiff's contention in the following language:

> "As matter of law the legal name of the defendant upon her marriage was Ethel M. Williams. The wife takes the husband's surname. . . . But it does not follow that, because the motor car was registered in the name of Mrs. John P. Williams, it was illegally registered. A woman whose husband is prominent in public life is

frequently known by her husband's name with the prefix 'Mrs.' In some instances married women conduct business in the husband's name; not infrequently a married woman is known and identified under the given name and surname of the husband and signs her name in this way with the prefix 'Mrs.' The defendant usually signed her name 'Mrs. John P. Williams'. She probably was better known under this name and could easily be identified by such a designation. . . . It has been held that a motor vehicle may be legally registered under a trade name. . . It is not intimated that that the defendant used her husband's name for the purpose of concealing her identity. She registered her vehicle in the name adopted by her. When signing she gave her correct address. She could easily be identified, and the purpose of the statute was complied with." (265 Mass. 661, 164 N.E. 444)

In the state of Illinois, a woman attorney practiced her profession for many years before her marriage and, of course, voted under her maiden name during that period. After her marriage, she continued to practice law and other business affairs under her maiden name with the consent of her husband. An action was brought by the state to cancel her registration as a voter because she had not registered under her married name, that is, her husband's surname. The court said that in view of the precise statutory provision which required reregistration on marriage, her maiden name would be cancelled from the registration records. The court noted that by common law principles and immemorial custom a woman upon her marriage abandons her maiden name and takes the husband's surname with which is used her own given name. The statute requiring reregistration expressly recognizes a change of name by marriage, and since, said the court,

> "it is only in the case of married women that there is any recognized custom or rule of law whereby marriage effects a change of name, it must logically follow that when the Legislature expressly referred to the fact that the name of a registered voter might be changed by marriage it had in mind the long established custom, policy and rule of the common law among English-speaking peoples whereby a woman's name is changed

by marriage and her husband's surname becomes as a matter of law her surname." (327 Ill. Ap. 63, 63 N.E. (2) 642)

[Recent cases have disputed this view. In the Stuart case (295 A. (2) (Md.) 233) the court lists those states that follow the rule that marriage changes a woman's surname by law, and those states that permit a woman to retain her maiden name after marriage if it is done "openly, notoriously and exclusively" subsequent to the marriage.]

In Florida, an action was brought to recover money and the declaration (or, as it is called in some states, the complaint) named the defendant as "Mrs. Francis M. Phelan, Sr., also known as Mrs. K. Phelan, as also Mrs. Katherine E. Phelan." One of the questions which the court was called upon to determine was whether it was a necessary inference from the declaration that the defendant at the time was a married woman. In the course of its opinion, the Florida court made the following observations:

"The prefix 'Mrs.' shows undoubtedly that at some time the defendant had been married to one Francis M. Phelan, Sr. Such prefix is not a name, but a mere title that usually distinguishes the person referred to as a married woman. However, it is not used exclusively by married women. . . . It is also used, and properly so, by widows and divorcees who make 'too large a number' to warrant us in holding that the title of 'Mrs.,' placed before the name of 'Francis M. Phelan, Sr.,' raises a presumption in law that the defendant is a married woman." (100 Fla. 1164, 131 So. 117) (See also 106 Cal. App. 623, 290 P. 146.)

In a case which is somewhat similar to the case we discussed earlier in this chapter, it appeared that the plaintiff, a woman, married in 1921 and in 1923 registered her car under her maiden name. Thereafter she and her husband were injured in an automobile accident, and she brought an action for damages. The Massachusetts court refused to allow her to recover on the ground that the car was not properly registered and was a nuisance on the highway. The court said that as a matter of law, after the plaintiff's marriage her legal surname was that of her husband; therefore, when she applied for registration of the automobile she did so in a name that was not hers. Since the statute governing such matters contemplates that a motor vehicle shall be registered in the name of its owner, the car was not legally registered at the time of the accident and so she was not entitled to recover. (256 Mass. 30, 152 N.E. 35)

In West Virginia a legal proceeding was brought, among other things, to strike certain names from an election petition because the names had prefixed to them certain titles.

The court denied the request in the following words:

"In law, a name is only a means of identification of a person, and a descriptive prefix or title clearly does not vitiate it. As the name is only matter of identification, a married woman may use in her signature, as her Christian name, some or all of her maiden name, or describe herself by the use of her husband's name with the prefix 'Mistress.' "(90 W. Va. 105, 110 S.E. 482)

[The word "Mrs." has undergone a partial metamorphosis as a result of the women's rights movement of the late sixties and the seventies having found in this respected form of address an affront to the individuality of women. Although no cases or laws relate to this matter, these modern suffragettes insist on using the prefix "Ms." Ms. replaces "Miss" and "Mrs.," and is the equivalent of Mr. The rationale for this is explainable. With new life styles adopted by the young, the aura of respectability associated with marriage suspect as a coverup for seriatim alliances and deceit, singles apartment houses mushrooming, the new phenomenom of groupies, cohabitation in college dormitories, society considering it chic to see "blue" movies such as Deep Throat and Last Tango in Paris, the laws of many states being changed so as to ignore any and all activities between or among consenting adults done in private, and the increased number of women who are entering the higher echelons of the business and professional world and wish to retain their maiden name to exclusively identify themselves, it is understandable that a new form of address would be introduced to reflect the new roles of women. While there is a good deal of resistance to this "new" woman (and Mrs. is still the more common prefix used by married, divorced and widowed women) by both sexes, if there is a common law right to change one's name at will, there is certainly no legal restraint as to the prefix one may use so long as there is no intent to deceive or defraud.

Legal complications can arise. If a husband and wife register in a hotel using their separate names, can a hotel refuse them accomodations? Probably not if proof of marriage can be established. (A copy of the marriage certificate will do, but unless you are looking for trouble, call in advance.) (See also Appendix E.)

The use of Ms. as a prefix is only a halfway goal to those who consider gender a meaningless distinction among human beings. Not only meaningless, but also demeaning to women and inhibiting their attempts for equal consideration in the world of achievement. To those who accept this view, possibly Ms. is merely the beginning of eliminating any sex distinction in a name. Not only will Ms., Mrs., Miss, Mr., and their variation go, but also first names that imply the sex of their bearers. Somewhere in our past society opted for sex distinctions in names; sometime in the future it could change this practice and hasten the ultimate revolution and all that it entails -- unisex.

One must digress at this point and note that this change may have more effect on language than law. As Russell Baker points out in "Nopersonlature" (Nomenclature [New York Times, Sec. 4, March 4, 1973, p. 13]), "chairman" will become "chairperson," and the suffix "man" ("The proper study of personkind is person," as Baker facetiously puts it) and its equivalents to represent humankind will be eradicated. It was more than a collegiate prank that inspired the Harvard Hasty Pudding Club to announce that its 1972 "Person of the Year" was Gloria Steinem. Like all changes, there is much to satirize and ridicule, but unless we are prepared to say that the millenium has been reached in society, then we must be prepared to consider all suggestions for reaching it.]

A married woman, seeking to be naturalized, requested the federal court to have her naturalization certificate issued to her in her maiden name instead of in her married name. The reasons she gave for this request were that she was a professional musician and was known professionally by her maiden name, that she feared that financial loss would result to her if her naturalization certificate showed her husband's surname instead of her maiden name, and that there would be a discrepancy between the musical union card she possessed and the naturalization certificate if the latter showed her husband's name. The court, however, denied her request, stating that the certificate of naturalization should indicate the name of her husband as belonging to the petitioner. The court also pointed out that the union card should conform to the naturalization certificate rather than that the certificate should be made to conform to the card. The court was not convinced that any loss would accrue to the petitioner if the certificate were issued in the surname of her husband, and expressly noted that under the law of New York a woman at marriage takes the surname of her husband, which becomes her legal name, and she ceases to be known by her maiden name. "By that name she must sue and be sued, make and take grants and execute all legal documents. Her maiden surname is absolutely lost, and she ceases to be known thereby." (9 Fed. Sup. 176)

[Despite the above quotation, there is no express stipulation in New York law requiring a woman to adopt the name of her husband. It is also questionable, in this author's opinion, and despite hoary New York case law to the contrary, that there is any common law mandate requiring a woman to take the name of her husband. While not authoritative, an article in the New York Post (Dec. 26, 1972, p. 47) quotes the New York City marriage clerk as saying, "There is nothing in the domestic relations law requiring a woman to take her husband's name." In fact, couples in New York do marry and retain their separate names. If it was the custom for New York women to adopt their husband's name it is now the custom for many of them not to do so.

The glory of the common law is its ability to change with the times. Ancient common law concepts (i.e. judge-made) thought irrevocable, such as caveat emptor, the concept of privity, the holder in due course doctrine, and sovereign immunity, have been modified by an enlightened judiciary despite diehard cries that the court is legislating. If it was not legislation to require a woman to adopt the name of her husband, then it is certainly not legislation for any court to reverse itself and acknowledge that women are entitled to the same considerations in changing their names as men.

Of course, as Appendix E illustrates, there are bills being proposed in state courts to remedy the situation without relying on the courts. (The court cannot act unless a case comes before it; the efficacy of legislation is that it can remove doubts without burdensome and expensive litigation.) Also, there are federal laws and a proposed Constitutional amendment that aim toward eradicating this atavistic appendage to the marital relationship.

However, if a woman commits herself to her husband's surname upon marriage (i.e., by custom), then she has accepted it for legal purposes (i.e., by signing the marriage certificate using her husband's surname, by accepting credit in his name, etc.). In a petition for a change of name, a married woman in Massachusetts applied to have a surname distinct from that of her husband. The application was granted. (See 1971 Annual Survey of Massachusetts Law 570.) The implications can be seen in this quotation from the article:

> "Ms. Sloane's request was unusual. The name-change procedure is normally utilized by a woman to reacquire her maiden name following a divorce; Ms. Sloane, however, had not been divorced nor was she contemplating divorce. Although a member of an on-going family group, she wanted a last name different from that of the other members of the group. As illustrated by Sloane, the court's request for the husband's assent to the wife's name change has become a standard feature of such proceedings. It is submitted that no interest of the state can be identified in the procedural requirement that a husband assent to the wife's change of name. It is not a valid exercise of judicial discretion to require a woman to bear a name that she does not want, unless there is a demonstrable administrative reason therefor. At present, a woman's child may bear a surname different from his mother's after the mother has undergone a divorce and remarriage; and no detrimental administrative consequences appear to result if the parties to a marriage choose to have different surnames. On the other hand, a growing number of women now believe it to be in their personal interest to express their individuality by the resumption or retention of their maiden names. A woman ought to be free to use her maiden name as a matter of right, subject only to her satisfying whatever procedural requirements are deemed necessary for administrative reasons. Enabling legislation is needed and should be enacted to this end." (p. 571)

Women who use their maiden names after marriage also have a problem in obtaining credit. It is difficult enough for a married woman to obtain credit in her married name separately from her husband (see Kellog, "Giving Credit Where Credit is Long Overdue," Woman's Day, Feb., 1973, p. 50), but the problem is compounded when the request is made in a name other than that of the husband. For tax and business purposes, it is important the a career woman -- or any woman with credit credentials -- have a separate identity from that of her husband. As the Kellog article points out, the road to this right may only come with political lobbying, legislation and the Equal Rights Amendment.

What should be the role of the courts as these situations come to light? Should they rely on ancient precedents? At the very least they should heed the accusation of Professors Johnston and Knapp: "they have [as a whole] failed to bring to sex discrimination cases those judicial virtues of detachment, reflection and critical analysis which have served them so well with respect to other sensitive social issues." (Sex Discrimination By Law: A Study in Judicial Perspective, 46 N.Y.U.L. Rev. 675, at 676 (1971)]

In the beginning of this chapter we discussed the general common law principles relating to the solidarity of husband and wife as those principles were developed in England and adopted in this country. However, not all the American states adopted the English common law (see the bibliography for elaboration on this common law principle); a number of them base their jurisprudence upon the principles of law known as the "civil law" which derived originally from Rome and came to this country by way of France and Spain. What this difference may mean is seen in a Texas case where a husband and wife executed their joint promissory note for money loaned to the husband. The particular facts of the case need not be gone into here, but the language of the court may be of interest. The court's opinion reads in part as follows:

> "There is a sound reason why the courts of this state should have a different conception of the disabilities of coverture from courts in states which have unqualifiedly adopted the common law principles governing marital rights. Our laws upon that subject did not have their origin in the common law, but were derived mainly from the civil law brought from Spain, Mexico and thence to the Republic of Texas. The common law theory that the legal existence of the wife was merged in the husband was not a principle of the

civil law and has never been recognized in this state."
(126 Tex. 69, 84 S.W. (2) 993)

The name used by a woman is very frequently an evidentiary fact which is taken into consideration with other circumstances to prove or disprove her marital condition, that is, to determine whether she was or was not in fact married.

In a proceeding for the administration of the estate of a deceased person in the state of Iowa, it appeared that the deceased woman had at one time used the prefix "Mrs." before her name, and an attempt was made to show that this meant that she had been previously married. But the court held that the mere fact that the appellation "Mrs." appeared before a woman's name did not alone constitute evidence that she had been married. (228 Ia. 75, 290 N.W. 13)

In another case, involving an estate also, it was necessary for the court to ascertain whether there existed a marriage between two certain persons, and on this point evidence was offered to establish the existence of the marriage. In discussing the proof which was presented to it, the court made the following comments:

> "Neither is the marriage disproved by the fact that in her business life and employment the appellant used her maiden name and at times registered herself as single. These facts are, of course, to be taken into consideration as bearing upon the primary fact; but are not conclusive." (253 A.D. 905, 2 N.Y.S. (2) 29)

In another New York litigation, an action was brought to revoke letters of administration, and the issues raised the question of the validity of a common law marriage between the decedent and a certain woman, and also the legitimacy of their child. The court pointed out that there was a presumption of the validity of the marriage and the fact that the woman had received family relief in her former name was not sufficient evidence to overcome this presumption (290 N.Y.S. 76, 160 Misc. 474)

In an Ohio case it seems that a man and woman had held themselves to be man and wife, that is that they had entered into a "common-law" marriage. It also appeared that the so-called husband had given to the woman notes which were made payable to her not under the husband's surname but under the name used by her before the alleged marriage. This was held to be some evidence that as between themselves the parties did not consider themselves to be married. (1 Oh. Sup. 321, 33 N.E. (2) 417)

[What are the rights of a married woman who objects to her husband's petition to change his name? One Isaiah Taminosian was admitted into the religion of Island under the name of Mohammed Nadir, which he wished to make his legal name. The petitioner's wife protested, and the court, in its discretion, upheld the wife. The dissenting opinion interpreted the change of name statute as merely formalizing the common law, by which the petitioner could change his name at will. Anticipating the cry of women's liberation some sixty years ahead of his time, this judge saw no reason in law that a man could not change his name, and if it pleases him, not include his wife in the change. (97 Neb. 514, 150 N.W. 824)

As has been mentioned previously, state law is controlling in this area of law. Alabama, it is clear, requires a woman to change her surname to that of her husband. In Hawaii, legislation makes it so. Many jurisdictions have never ruled on this point. (Consult the Appendices -- particularly A and D. Also check with the clerk of the court, or have your lawyer do so.) In many instances, lower court rulings prevail and they do not have the force of precedent. Also, as pointed out in Appendix E, many legislatures have before them proposals to remove this matter from the discretion of the court and make of the change of name statutes what they should be -- a formal way of changing one's name that simply furthers the common law method.

Lastly, the Equal Rights Amendment has passed Congress and needs the approval of three-quarter of the states (twenty-nine have ratified as of this writing)   to become the Twenty-Seventh Amendment to the Constitution. Some scholars interpret the passage of this amendment as doing away with any limitations of women to change their names as presently imposed.

In an excellent compilation, "Impact Study of the Equal Rights Amendment," (1973), Charlene M. Taylor and Stuart Herzog suggest that the amendment will not only give a divorcing woman freedom to assume a name other than that contracted for in marriage (as stipulated by the laws in most states), but also will give this option to both parties to the marriage (p. 59).]

Chapter 8

BUSINESS NAMES

In Chapter Five we discussed the use of assumed or fictitious names by individuals or partnerships and the statutory requirements of the several states which provide that persons doing business under such names must register them with the appropriate state or county official. In this chapter we will consider in a more general way the names assumed by business enterprises and especially of corporations. Necessarily, the treatment of the subject will be brief, considering the scope of this book. For a run-down of the law of all jurisdictions relating to corporations, partnerships, trademarks and tradenames, see 5 Martindale-Hubbell Law Directory (1973) and the Corporation Manual (both can be found in many large public libraries).

In a famous case known as the Dartmouth College case, which was decided in the United States Supreme Court in 1819, Chief Justice Marshall gave the following definition of a corporation:

> "A corporation is an artificial being, invisible, intangible and existing only in contemplation of law. Being the mere creature of law, it possesses only those properties which the charter of its creation confers upon it, either expressly or as incidental to its very existence. These are such as are supposed best calculated to effect the object for which it was created. Among the most important are immortality, and if the expression may be allowed, individuality; properties by which a perpetual succession of many persons are considered as the same, and may act as a single individual." (4 Wheat. (U.S.) 518)

A corporation is, of course, made up of numerous individuals, known as the stockholders, but the corporation itself is treated as if it were an independent person separate and distinct from its members. Since a corporation is, as quoted above, a "mere creature of law," it takes its origin from the laws of the state and cannot be created unless it is organized in accordance with such laws. Such organization is accomplished by filing with the proper state official, such as the secretary of state, a document known as the certificate of incorporation or articles of incorporation, which is executed by a minimum number of "incorporators" as provided by the particular state statute. In addition to other matters which must appear in the corporate charter, there must be present the name which will be borne by the corporation and by which it will conduct its business transactions. Associated with the corporate name is its seal, which should be affixed to all documents executed by the corporation, certainly the most important ones, although nowadays, the use of a seal is less widespread than formerly.

As with the name of an individual, the name assumed by a business enterprise, whether conducted as a partnership or corporation, has for its chief purpose the identification of the entity conducting the business. The artificial names assumed by an individual or partnership are usually set forth in the business certificate which the state laws demand must be filed. The name assumed by a corporation is stated in the articles of incorporation.

Obviously, dealings with a corporation would be almost impossible unless it bore a name. The seal of the corporation bears upon it the corporate name, the state in which the corporation was incorporated, and the year of incorporation, and, as stated above, should be impressed upon all corporate documents.

The choice of a name for a business enterprise often presents problems, whether the business is to be conducted as a corporation or otherwise. Generally speaking, the name to be adopted may be any name, subject, however, to certain restrictions based upon morality and good taste. An obscene name, for instance, would not be permitted. In addition, the persons engaged in the business will try to choose a name which sound business policy makes advisable. If an individual or a partnership has conducted business for many years and has built up a valuable reputation and good will, obviously, should it desire to incorporate thereafter, it will try to use the same name as the corporate name. This can usually be done by taking the individual or partnership name and merely adding thereto the words "Incorporated" or "Corporation," or their abbreviations, "Inc." or "Corp."

In addition to the general restrictions upon a corporate

name which we have noted, the state statutes often impose other limitations. For example:

> "No certificate of incorporation of a proposed domestic corporation . . . having the same name as a corporation authorized to do business under the laws of this state, or a name so nearly resembling it as to be calculated to deceive, shall be filed or recorded . . .; nor shall any corporation . . . be authorized to do business in this state unless its name has such word or words, abbreviation, affix or prefix therein or thereto, as will clearly indicate that it is a corporation as distinguished from a natural person, firm or co-partnership . . ."

An example of the type of conflict that can result from corporate name changes is illustrated by a federal court permitting Crowell Collier and Macmillan, Inc., a New York publishing concern to change its name to Macmillan, Inc. Macmillan, Ltd. of London argued that the name change would cause "worldwide conflict and confusion" and would violate the Trade-Mark Act of 1946. (New York Times, Dec. 5, 1972; N.Y. L.J., Dec. 5, 1972, p. 1) This case was pending at the time of publication of this volume, but it points up the legal and financial problems of corporate giants, as well as the very simple problem of business identification.

The laws of most states also prohibit a corporation from using as part of its name the words "bank," "banking," "trust," "savings," "finance," "insurance," and other similar words unless the corporation is organized under the banking or insurance laws. Also, the words "doctor" or "lawyer" may be forbidden, unless the corporation is a nonprofit membership corporation. A statute of the United States provides that a banking institution may not use the word "national" in its name unless it is organized under the federal banking act. The use of the word "engineering" may also be restricted.

In addition to the words "Incorporated" and "Corporation," and their abbreviations, a corporation may also use the term "Limited," abbreviated "Ltd." to show its corporate existence. In some states the word "Company" is permitted to show that a corporation is intended, although in other states, e.g., New York, such word is insufficient, since it is also used by individuals and partnerships.

Although New York law does not permit a corporation to

take a name already used by a domestic corporation (that is, one organized in New York) or by a foreign corporation (that is, one organized outside of the state) if the latter is authorized to do business in New York, many states impose no restrictions so far as the name of a foreign corporation is concerned, whether doing business in the state or not.

It may happen that after the corporate enterprise has engaged in business for a period of time, it may appear advisable to change the corporate name. While, as we have seen, individuals may almost universally change their name without permission of a court, the change of name of a corporation can be effected only by filing a special certificate, and it must appear that the change has been authorized by the stockholders or by the directors, as the particular state statute may provide.

Sometimes a corporation, after its organization, may wish to conduct its business under one or more other names which differ from its authorized corporate name. In some states, for example South Carolina (190 S.C. 367) and Idaho (58 Ida. 578, 76 P. (2) 438), it would seem that a corporation may, in the absence of a statute prohibiting such action, be known by several names and its contracts may be enforced by either party. But in other jurisdictions, as in Georgia (52 Ga. App. 434) and New York (172 Misc. 595, 15 N.Y.S. (2) 506) it appears that a corporation may not conduct business under an assumed name and may be prevented from recovering on contracts made in such name.

We will close this chapter with a case, decided in New York, which shows how a state may limit the use of a proposed name. Similar situations may be found in all the states. In this particular case, a number of persons wished to establish a corporation to be known as "We Americans, Inc." It appears that the purpose of the organization was to preserve and promote American ideals and principles. However, the right to use this was refused, since, in the opinion of the court, all American citizens were entitled to the use of this term and it could not be restricted to one group. (166 Misc. 167, 2 N.Y.S. (2) 235)

Readers are advised to consult such texts as Hornstein on corporation law for more complete and authoritative information.

APPENDICES

Appendix A

SUMMARY OF STATE LAWS RELATING TO CHANGE OF NAME

ALABAMA: Declaration for change of name is filed in the Probate Court showing the reasons for the change.

STATUTE

Ala. Code t. 13, § 278 (1958)

ALASKA: "A person may bring an action for change of name in the superior court. No change of name of a person except a woman upon her marriage or divorce shall be made unless the court finds sufficient reasons for the change and also finds it consistent with the public interest."

STATUTE

Alaska Stat. §09.55.010 (1962)

ARIZONA: Application is filed in Superior Court of county of residence, setting forth reasons for change. Minor over sixteen years may file his own application. Court may order publication or service of notice upon interested parties. Change does not release applicant from obligation nor destroy rights of property or action. Final divorce decree may change the wife's name.

STATUTE

Ariz. Rev. Stat. Ann. §12-601, 12-602 (1956)

ARKANSAS: Application is filed in Chancery and Circuit Courts, showing good reasons for change. Thereafter applicant shall be known, sue and be sued, by the new name. The court may restore her maiden name to a divorced wife if no children were born to the dissolved marriage.

STATUTES

Ark. Stat. Ann. §34-801 to 34-803 (1947), §34-1216 (1947)

(divorce), § 82-507 (1960) (corrections)

CALIFORNIA: Petition is made to Superior Court of the county of residence. If the person is under eighteen years, the petition is made by the parent, guardian, relative or next friend. The petition must show reason for change.

STATUTES

Cal. Civ. Pro. §1275-1279 (West 1972), Cal. Civ. §1096 (West 1955) (deeds), Cal. Corp. § 3600 (West 1964), Cal. Elections §214 (West), Cal. Health and Safety §10460-10462 (West Supp. 1972) (amendment of birth records, naturalization)

COLORADO: Petition is filed in District, Superior, or County Court in the county of residence, setting forth reasons for change. The judge will order the change if satisfied it is proper and not detrimental to any person. Notice is to be published at least three times in the newspaper within twenty days after court order.

STATUTE

Colo. Rev. Stat. Ann. §20-1-1 (1963, Supp. 1965)

CONNECTICUT: Petition is made to Superior Court in the county of residence. Thereafter, the petitioner must be known by the name shown in the decree. A decree of divorce may provide for the change of name of the divorced wife. A person owning or having interest in real estate whose name is changed must within sixty days after such change file a certificate, acknowledged, giving old and new names.

STATUTES

Conn. Gen. Stat. Ann. § 52-11 (1958), § 45-69 (1958) (adoption), §46-21 (1958) (divorce), § 47-12 (1958), §47-12a (1973 Supp.) (real estate)

DELAWARE: Petition is made to Superior Court of the county of residence. Petition of a minor is signed by the parents or guardian; a minor over fourteen years must also sign petition. The petition must be published at least once a week for three weeks before filing. If there appears no reason for not granting the petition, it may be granted. On granting divorce to a woman, the court may allow the resumption of her maiden name or the name of a former deceased husband.

STATUTE

Del. Code Ann. tit. 10, § 5901-5905 (1953), 13, § 1536 (1953) (divorce)

DISTRICT OF COLUMBIA: A District resident files an application in the District Court of the United States for the District of Columbia, setting forth the reasons for change. An application of an infant is filed by the parent, guardian or next friend. The court has discretion to grant the petition. Notice of filing an application is published in the newspaper once a week for three consecutive weeks prior to the hearing. A divorce decree may restore to the wife her maiden name or other previous name.

STATUTE

D.C. Code Ann. § 16-2501-§ 16-2503 (1966), § 16-312 (1966) (adoption)

FLORIDA: The constitution prohibits the legislature from enacting special or local laws changing names of persons. Petition is filed in the Chancery Court of residence, showing new name, and the court shall decree that the change shall be made.

STATUTES

Fla. Stat. Ann. Const. Art. 3, § 11 (1969), § 62.031 (1969), § 104.24 (1960) (elections), § 97.103 (1972 Supp.) (registration), § 322.19 (1968) (license)

GEORGIA: Petition is filed with the Superior Court of the county of residence, showing reasons for change. The court may, in its discretion, authorize change, but nothing shall operate fraudulently to deprive another of his legal rights. Notice of filing is to be published once a week for four weeks to enable objections to be filed. A divorce decree may restore to the divorced wife the name she bore at the time of her last marriage.

STATUTE

Ga. Code Ann. §79-501 - §79-504 (1964, 1972 Supp.)

HAWAII: Change is made by decree based on petition. The petition of a minor is made by the parent or guardian. The petition must be published once in a newspaper. A judge may allow a divorced woman in the divorce decree to use her maiden name or the name of a former husband. Also, "Every married woman shall adopt her husband's name as a family name."

STATUTE

Hawaii Rev. Stat. § 574-1 to § 574-5 (1968)

IDAHO: Application is made to the District Court where the applicant resides. A petition by a male under twenty-one years or a female under eighteen years is filed by parent, guardian, near relative or next friend. Reason for change must be shown. The notice of the hearing is published for four successive weeks. Objections may be filed, and the court has discretion to grant or dismiss the application.

STATUTE

Idaho Code §7-801 (1948), §7-802 to 804 (1972 Supp.)

ILLINOIS: Petition is made to the Circuit Court of the county of residence. If no reason appears why prayer should be denied it will be granted. The petition of a minor is signed by the parent or guardian. The notice of application is published for three consecutive weeks, the first publication at least six weeks before petition is filed.

STATUTES

Ill. Ann. Stat. ch. 96, §1-10 (Smith-Hurd 1971), 40, §17 (Smith-Hurd 1956) (divorce), 46, §6-54 (Smith-Hurd 1966) (elections)

INDIANA: The petition is filed in the Circuit Court of the county of residence. The notice of filing petition must be published by three weekly publications, the last of which must be at least thirty days before the hearing. On granting a divorce, the court may allow a woman to resume her maiden name or previous married name, whether she be plaintiff or defendant in the divorce action.

STATUTE

Ind. Ann. Stat. § 3-801 to §3-805 (1968, 1972 Supp.), §29-3428 (1969) (elections)

IOWA: Any person who has attained majority may file a petition to change his name. He must be a resident of the county where the statement is filed. Reason for the change must be shown and real estate owned set forth. Statement is filed with the clerk of the District Court. No person may change name more than once, under the statute.

STATUTE

Iowa Code Ann. §674.1 - 674.14 (1973 Supp.)

KANSAS: Petition is filed in the District Court of the county of residence, showing reasons for change. Notice of hearing is published for three consecutive weeks. Hearings shall be at least thirty days after first publication. The court may order change if it appears reasonable. A divorced wife is entitled to resume her maiden or former name.

STATUTE

Kan. Stat. Ann. §60-1401 to §60-1403 (1964)

KENTUCKY: Petitioner must be eighteen and not a married woman, or must be an infant if petition is made by the parent or guardian. Petition is filed in the County Court of the county of residence. The court may restore to a wife obtaining divorce the name she bore before marriage.

STATUTE

Ken. Rev. Stat. Ann. §401.010 - §401.040 (1972), §403.060 (1972) (divorce), §117.735 (1971) (election)

LOUISIANA: Petition filed in District Court of parish of

residence. Petition of minor filed by parents, tutor or special tutor. Reasons for change must be shown. District Attorney must be served, and hearing is held.

STATUTE

La. Rev. Stat. § 13:4751 - 4755 (1968)

MAINE: Petition is addressed to the Judge of Probate of the county where the petitioner resides. The petition of a minor is made by the legal custodian. Notice must be given. A decree of divorce may provide for the change of name of the divorced wife.

STATUTE

Me. Rev. Stat. Ann. tit. 19, § 781 (1964), 19, § 752 (1964) (divorce)

MARYLAND: Petition is filed in the Court of Equity in the county of residence. Reasons for change must be shown. An infant's petition is filed by the parent or guardian.

STATUTE

Md. Ann. Code art. 16, § 123 (1957), 9B Md. Ann. Code. Md. Rules BH 70-75 (1957)

MASSACHUSETTS: The petition is heard in the Probate Court of the county of residence. Sufficient reason for change must be shown. Public notice of hearing is required. Birth record must be filed unless not obtainable. The court granting divorce to a woman may allow the resumption of her maiden name or that of former husband.

STATUTES

Mass. Ann. Laws ch. 210, §12 (1958), ch. 208, § 23 (1958) (divorce)

MICHIGAN: Probate Court may change the name of an adult who is resident for one year in the county. The petitioner must show sufficient reason and no fraudulent intent. The court shall order publication and hold a hearing. Another person with the same name can object to the petition. If the petitioner is a husband

70

or head of family, the name of his wife and minor child may be included in the decree. If the child is over sixteen he must file written consent. A divorced woman may be given her maiden name, the name of a prior marriage, or may adopt another name, unless there is a minor child of the marriage. Note: The provisions are superseded for persons over eighteen.

STATUTE

Mich. Comp. Laws §711.1, 711.2 (1968), §552.391 (1967) (divorce)

MINNESOTA: The constitution prohibits local laws changing names. The petitioner must be resident in the county for one year. The petition is filed in the District Court, and must describe lands in or on which the petitioner has interest or liens. Petition may include the name of the wife, if proper, or of a minor child. Petitioner must prove identity by two witnesses and if a minor, his guardian must appear. If there is intent to defraud, it is a misdemeanor. Where divorce action is brought by the woman, the decree of divorce may change her name.

STATUTE

Minn. Stat. Ann. §259.10, 259.11 (1971), §518.27 (1969) (divorce), §201.14 (1959) (elections)

MISSISSIPPI: Petition is filed in the Chancery Court of the county of residence.

STATUTE

Miss. Code Ann. § 1269-01, 1269-02 (1943)

MISSOURI: Petition is made to the Circuit Court of the county of residence. The reasons for the change must be shown and that it would not be detrimental to any other person. Notice of change is to be published three times within twenty days after the court order. When wife obtains divorce, the court may decree change of name to her maiden name or that of a former husband.

STATUTE

Mo. Rev. Stat. §527.270-527.290 (1959), 452.100 (1959) (divorce)

MONTANA: The constitution prohibits special laws changing names. Petition is filed in the District Court of the county of residence. If the petitioner is under twenty-one years the petition is filed by the parent or guardian. Reasons for change must be shown. Notice of hearing is to be published four successive weeks. Objections may be filed by interested persons.

STATUTE

Mont. Rev. Code Ann. § 93-100-1 (9964) to § 93-100-9 (9971) (1949, Supp. 1971)

NEBRASKA: The constitution forbids the legislature to enact special laws to change names. Petition is filed in the District Court of the county of residence, and must show reason for change. Petitioner must be a resident of the county for one year. Notice of filing the petition must be published for thirty days.

STATUTE

Neb. Rev. Stat. §61-101 to §61-104 (1971)

NEVADA: The constitution prohibits special laws changing names. Petition is made to the District Court of the district of residence. Notice of filing petition is to be published once a week for three successive weeks. If there are no objections and good reason appears, the court will order the change. If there are objections, a hearing is held. The court may change the name of a divorced wife.

STATUTE

Nev. Rev. Stat. §41.270 to §41.290 (1971)

NEW HAMPSHIRE: Petition is filed with the Probate Court of the county of residence. Petition will be granted if good cause is shown. A divorce decree may change the name of the wife to that borne by her before the last marriage. In limited divorces, "the name of the wife shall not be changed."

STATUTE

N.H. Rev. Stat. Ann. § 547:7 (1955), § 458:24 (1972 Supp.), § 458:27

NEW JERSEY: Petition is filed in the County Court of the county of residence or the Superior Court. The court may allow a divorced wife to resume any name used by her before the marriage and may order her to refrain from using her divorced husband's surname.

STATUTE

N.J. Rev. Stat. § 2A:52-1 to § 2A:52-4 (1952, 1972-73 Supp), § 2A:34-21 (1952)

NEW MEXICO: Petition is filed in the District Court of the district of residence by a person over fourteen years of age. Notice of making application is published once each week for two consecutive weeks.

STATUTE

N.M. Stat. Ann. § 22-5-1 to § 22-5-3 (1953)

NEW YORK: Petition to change name is filed in the County Court or in the Supreme Court of the county of residence. A resident of the City of New York may file petition in the Supreme Court or any branch of the Civil Court of the City of New York in any County. Petition of an infant is made by the next friend, parents or guardian. The petition must show the grounds of application and whether or not petitioner was convicted of a crime or adjudicated a bankrupt, whether or not any judgments or liens of record are recorded against him, whether or not any actions or proceedings are pending to which he is a party, describing same. A birth certificate, or certificate that none is available, must be attached. Notice of petition to change the name of an infant, showing when and where to be presented, must be served on the parents or guardian if any. Notice may be dispensed with by court if the person to be given notice cannot be located. The court will order the change of an infant's name if it appears the interests of the infant will be substantially promoted. Change of name takes effect not less than thirty days after entry of the order. The order must be published in a designated newspaper at least once within twenty days after entry thereof. The constitution prohibits private or local bills changing names.

STATUTE

N.Y. Civ. Rights § 60-63 (McKinney 1944, Supp. 1972)

NORTH CAROLINA: The constitution prohibits changes of names by private laws. Application is filed before the clerk of the Superior Court of the county of residence. Ten days notice thereof must be given by publication at the courthouse door. Application of a minor is made by the parent, guardian or next friend. Abandonment of child by one parent vitiates need for that parent's consent. Application must show good reason and if name was ever changed before. Must file proof of good character by two citizens. Order of change is issued by the clerk. Only one change is permitted under the statute, but petitioner may assume former name on application. A divorced wife may resume her maiden name or the name of a prior deceased husband on application to the clerk of the court of the county of residence.

STATUTE

N. Car. Gen. Stat. §101-1 to §101-7 (1972), §20-676 (1965) (registration), § 48-14 (1965) (adoption), §50-12 (1965) (divorce)

NORTH DAKOTA: Petition is filed in the District Court of the county of residence. Petioner must be a bona fide resident of the county for the preceding six months. Reasons for the change must be shown and thirty days prior notice of the application must be published.

STATUTE

N. Dak. Cent. Code Ann. § 32-28-01 to § 32-28-04 (1960, Supp. 1971), §14-11-11 (1960) (adoption)

OHIO: Petition is filed in the Court of Common Pleas or in the Probate Court of the county of residence. Petitioner must be a bona fide resident of the county for one year before filing the petition. Reasons for the change must be given and notice of the application must be published at least thirty days before the petition is filed. A minor (under twenty-one) must have the consent of both parents, or a hearing will be held in the matter. If a divorced wife so desires, the Court of Common Pleas can restore to her any name she had before the marriage.

STATUTE

Ohio Rev. Code Ann. § 2717.01 (Page 1954, Supp. 1972)

OKLAHOMA: The constitution prohibits special laws changing names. Petition may be filed in the District Court by a person domiciled in the state for more than three years and residing in the county for more than thirty days. The petition of a minor is filed by the guardian or next friend. The petition must show facts as to birth and reasons for the change; that it is not sought for illegal or fraudulent purposes or to delay or hinder creditors. Notice of filing is published for one week. It is a misdemeanor if change is sought for fraudulent reason. The remedy is exclusive; no change of name is permitted except as provided by the statute, or by marriage, decree of divorce, or adoption. If a divorce is granted because of the husband's fault, the court can restore her maiden name to the wife.

STATUTE

Okla. Stat. Ann. tit. 12, § 1631-1640 (1961)

OREGON: The constitution forbids local or special laws changing names. Petition is filed in the Probate Court or equivalent of the county of residence. Must show sufficient reasons. Public notice of the application must be given. The decree of the divorce court may also change the name of the divorced wife. Birth certificates of children will be changed upon change of name by the parent.

STATUTE

Ore. Rev. Stat. § 33.410 to §33.430 (1971)

PENNSYLVANIA: The petition is filed in the Court of Common Pleas of the county of residence. Reasons for the change must be given. The petitioner must set forth his residences for the preceding five years. The other spouse may join in the application. The application must show no judgments or decrees of record against the petitioner. Notice of filing to be published in two newspapers. Objections may be heard. It is unlawful to assume a different name except by court proceedings. A divorced woman may resume her maiden name by filing acknowledged notice with the prothonotary of the court where the divorce was entered.

STATUTE

Pa. Stat. Ann. tit. 54, §1-6 (1964), 25, §623-4(b) (1969) (elections), 57, §156 (1964) (notary)

RHODE ISLAND: The Probate Court has jurisdiction to change the names of persons. A woman to whom a divorce has been decreed may be authorized by the decree of divorce to change her name.

STATUTE

R.I. Gen. Laws. Ann. §8-9-9 (1970), §15-5-17 (1970) (divorce), §15-7-4 (1970) (adoption), §15-7-15 (1970) (adoption)

SOUTH CAROLINA: The constitution prohibits special legislation affecting change of names. Petition is exhibited to a judge of the Circuit Court showing reasons for change. The court may allow a divorced wife to resume her maiden name or the name of any former husband.

STATUTE

S. Car. Code Ann. §48-51 to §48-55 (1962, Supp. 1971), §10-2584 (1962) (adoption), §15-1382 (1962) (adoption), § 20-5.2 (1962) (legitimacy)

SOUTH DAKOTA: Petitioner must be a resident of the county for six months. Petition is filed in the Circuit Court of the county and reasons for change must be shown. Notice of hearing must be published once each week for two successive weeks. A decree of divorce may restore to a divorced wife her maiden name or the name she legally bore before the marriage, unless she was granted the custody of a minor child.

STATUTE

S.D. Compiled Laws Ann. § 21-37-1 to § 21-37-10 (1967, 1972 Supp.), §12-4-18 (1967) (elections)

TENNESSEE: Application is made by a resident of the county in which application is made to the appropriate Circuit, Probate and County Court. Reasons for the proposed change must be set forth in the petition.

STATUTE

Tenn. Code Ann. § 23-801 to § 23.805 (1955, 1972 Supp.), § 36-304 (1955) (legitimacy), § 36-105 (1972 Supp.) (adoption)

TEXAS: The constitution prohibits special laws changing names. Application is filed in the District Court of the county of residence showing reasons for change. Application of a minor is filed by the guardian or next friend. Change shall not release the petitioner from responsibilities or destroy the rights of third persons. A divorce decree may change the name of either party if requested.

STATUTE

Tex. Rev. Civil Stat. art. 5928-5931 (1962)

UTAH: The constitution prohibits change of names by special laws. Petition is filed in the District Court of the county of residence, showing reasons for the change. The petitioner must be a resident of the county for one year prior to filing the petition. The court may order notice of hearing.

STATUTE

Utah Code Ann. § 42-1-1, 42-1-3 (1970), §78-30-10 (1953) (adoption)

VERMONT: The instrument stating change of name is signed, sealed and acknowledged before a judge of the Probate Court in the district of residence. A married person must have the consent of the spouse in such instrument, who must also sign, seal and acknowledge it. The change of name by a married man automatically changes the names of his wife and minor children. (§814). A form of the statement is set forth in the statute. It must show the place of birth and names and birthplaces of minor children. The petition of a minor is signed by persons acting for him, but if he is over fourteen years old he must consent. Notice of filing is published three successive weeks in newspaper. A certificate of change is filed with the original birth record of the applicant and of his minor children. The original marriage record is also changed. On granting divorce to a woman, the court may allow her to resume her maiden name or the name of a former husband. The court may change the names of minor children of divorced parents if requested in the libel for divorce.

STATUTE

Vt. Stat. Ann. tit. 15, § 811-816 (1958, Supp. 1972), tit. 15, § 557 (1958) (divorce), tit. 15, § 558 (1958) (divorce-minors), tit. 15, § 431 (1958) (adoption)

VIRGINIA: Application is filed in the Circuit Court of the county or the Circuit or Corporation Court of the corporation in which the petitioner resides, or in the Circuit Court of the City of Richmond. A minor's application is made by the parent, guardian or next friend. The court, in its discretion, may order the change of name. An unlawful change of name is a misdemeanor. A decree of divorce may allow a divorced wife to resume her maiden name. The constitution prohibits special legislation changing names.

STATUTE

Va. Code Ann. § 8.577.1 (1957), § 24.1-51 (1972 Supp.) (elections), § 55-106.1 (1957) (divorce), § 63.1-221 (1972 Supp) (adoption)

WASHINGTON: The constitution prohibits special legislation changing names. Petition is filed in the Superior Court of the county of residence. Reasons for the change must be shown. The petitioner may request the change of name of his child or ward. The court may, for just and reasonable cause, change the name of a divorced woman by decree or order.

STATUTE

Wash. Rev. Code Ann. § 4.24.130 (1962), § 26.08.130 (1961)

(divorce), § 29.10.050 (1965) (elections)

WEST VIRGINIA: The petitioner may change his name or the name of his child or ward by filing petition in the Circuit Court or any other court of record having jurisdiction of the county in which he resides, or the judge thereof in vacation. The petitioner must be a bona fide resident of the county for one year before filing the petition. Reasons for the change must be shown. Before filing, the petitioner must publish notice of making the application. Objections may be filed and heard. Unlawful change of name is a misdemeanor. On granting divorce to a woman, the court may, if there are no children of the marriage, allow the wife to resume her maiden name or the name of a former deceased husband.

STATUTE

W. Vir. Code Ann. §48-5-1 to §48-5-6 (1966, 1972 Supp.), §48-4-1 (1972 Supp.) (adoption)

WISCONSIN: Petition of a minor or an adult is filed in the Circuit Court or County Court of the county of residence. If a minor is under fourteen years, petition is made by the parents or guardian. Copy of order of change is filed with the register of deeds and with the registrar of vital statistics if the petitioner was born in the state. The birth and marriage records shall show new name. Change of name is restricted where petitioner is practicing a profession under a license unless a hearing establishes that no detriment will result. A public school teacher is not subject to this restriction. Notice of making application is published according to statutory requirements for notice. After granting a divorce the court may permit the wife to resume her maiden name only if she receives no alimony; and if there are children of the marriage, she may be permitted to resume her such name if her parental rights to the children of the marriage have been terminated.

STATUTE

Wis. Stat. Ann. § 296.36, 296.37 (Supp. 1972), § 48.91 (Supp. 1972) (adoption), § 247.20 (Supp. 1972) (divorce)

WYOMING: Petition to change name is filed in the District

Court of the county of residence. Reasons for the change must be shown. The petitioner must be a resident of the county for two years before filing the petition. Public notice of the making of the petition must be given in the same manner as service by publication on nonresidents in civil actions.

STATUTE

Wyo. Stat. Ann. §1-739 to §1-742 (1959)

FORMS

The forms in Appendix B were made available by Matthew Bender and Co. and are from Bender's Forms for the Consolidated Laws, which provide forms arranged by code section of the laws of New York. The set may be available in large public libraries or in a law library (there are similar form books for other states). Readers are cautioned that changes in the law could conceivably affect the content of these forms. Consult the latest supplement to this set, and, preferably, an attorney. The material in this section is under copyright (c) 1972, by Matthew Bender & Company, Inc., and reprinted with permission from Bender's Forms for the Consolidated Laws.

SECTION 60   FORM 1

Petition for Change of Name

.... COURT—............ County

In the Matter of the Application of	Petition
....	
for leave to change his name to	Index No. ....
....	

TO THE .... COURT, COUNTY OF ....:

............, by this petition, alleges:

1. My name is ....

2. The name which I propose to assume is ....

3. My residence is at ...., *Borough of* ...., New York.

4. I am of the age of ...... years, having been born on ...., 19... at ...., New York, *and annexed hereto is my birth certificate (or,—and annexed hereto is a certificate of .... that a certificate of my birth is not available.)* I am by occupation a ...., being now employed as a .... by .... at ...., New York.

(4a. Your petitioner is not a member of any armed forces or merchant marine, nor inducted for any military or naval service. He is not registered and not required to be registered under the United States Selective Service Act. (*Or*—He is, however duly registered under said name of .... with Local Board No. .... of United States Selective Service, at .... Street, ..., New York.))

5. I am a citizen of the U. S., (having been duly naturalized on ...., 19..., in the U. S. District Court, for the .... District of New York.)

6. I am (single and have never been married).

7. I have never been convicted of a crime (except ....).

8. There are no judgments or liens of record against me or against any property in my name. There is no action or proceeding pending to which I am a party. I have never been adjudicated a bankrupt. In fact, no proceeding in bankruptcy has ever been instituted by or against me in any court or before any officer of the state or of the United States nor have I at any time made an assignment for the benefit of creditors. There are no claims, demands, liabilities, or obligations on a written instrument or otherwise against me or to which I am a party. I have no creditors and no person will be adversely affected or prejudiced in any way by the proposed change of name.

9. The grounds of this application are as follows: *(Set forth reasons why change of name is sought, as for instance:*—Your petitioner desires to change his name and proposes to assume the name of .... It is desirable for the petitioner to change his name because his present name, ..., is, as

plainly to be seen, cumbersome and has led to a great deal of confusion and embarrassment, and the use of such name by your petitioner will continue to cause much confusion and embarrassment. One cannot readily spell or pronounce the petitioner's present name. The fact of the matter is that your petitioner is engaged in the insurance and real estate business at ...., New York. In his business, it is necessary that he continually make new contacts and acquaintances. Upon being introduced to strangers, they are unable to readily grasp your petitioner's name, or the spelling thereof. Also people are continually misspelling petitioner's name in connection with communications written to him. Many letters sent to your petitioner have been misdirected or returned to the sender because of a misspelling of your petitioner's name. All of the foregoing has resulted in a great loss to your petitioner, both in business and in friendship.)

(*Or:*—Your petitioner was brought up from infancy by ...., and never knew until recently that he had any name other than that of the family name of said .... He always went by the name of .... All his friends, associates, and neighbors and the people in the community knew and still know him by the name of .... It was not until ...., 19... that he was informed that his real name was ...., this latter name being the name appearing on his birth certificate and under which he was baptised. Even since acquiring such information, he has, however, continued to be known by the name of .... and has continued to be so known by his friends, neighbors and in the community. The petitioner works for .... and is employed by said person under the name of .... and is known by that name among his fellow workmen and to his foreman. They do not know him by any other name. Recently he had occasion to take title to two certain parcels of real property and in this connection his attorney advised his taking the same in his real name, to wit, the name of ...., and this was done, but such use of said name has caused great confusion, because he has never been known by that name. Under all the circumstances, it is fitting and proper that he be given legally the name of .... so that people will not be misled, and in this connection the said .... and the members of the family of said .... with whom the petitioner has been brought up have no objection to his assuming the name of ....)

10. No previous application has been made for this relief.

WHEREFORE, your petitioner respectfully prays that an order be granted permitting him to assume the name ....

Dated, ..., 19....

....
Petitioner

....
Attorney for Petitioner

....
Telephone Number ....

STATE OF NEW YORK, ⎰ ss.:
County of ...., ⎱

............, being duly sworn, deposes and says that he is the person named in and making this foregoing petition; that the same is true as to his own knowledge except as to those matters therein stated to be alleged on information and belief and as to those matters he believes it to be true.

....

Sworn to before me this
...... day of ...., 19....

SECTION 60   FORM 3

Petition for Change of Name of Infant

.... Court—............ County

In the Matter of the Application for
the Change of Name
of
........................,
an infant,
By ...., his general
guardian (or, guardian of his person, next friend, father, mother.)

Petition

Index No. ....

To the .... Court, County of ...., New York:

The petition of ...., respectfully shows:

1. Petitioner resides at .... Street, ...,
New York.

2. *(Show petitioner's relationship to infant, as for instance:—)*
Petitioner is the General Guardian (or, guardian of the person;
next friend; father; mother, of the above named ...., an
infant. (Petitioner was duly appointed the general guardian (*or*,
guardian of the person) of the said infant by a decree of the Surrogate's Court of the County of ...., rendered on or about
the ...... day of ...., 19..., and is now duly qualified
and acting as such guardian.)

3. *(Show whether father and mother are living, etc., as for
instance:—)*   The father of the said infant, to wit, one ......

...... who formerly resided at .... Street, ..., New York, is deceased, having died a resident of .... on or about the ...... day of ...., 19... (and the mother of the said infant, to wit, ..., formerly of .... Street, ..., New York, is also deceased, having died a resident of .... on or about the ...... day of ...., 19....) (There has been no appointment of a general guardian or guardian of the person of said infant.)

4. The present name of the said infant is .... and the name which it is proposed that the said infant shall assume is ....

5. The said infant resides at .... Street, ..., New York, with .... who is the (uncle) of the said infant.

6. The said infant is of the age of ...... years, having been born in ...., New York, on the ...... day of ...., 19..., (and a certificate of his birth is hereto annexed) (or,— and annexed hereto is a certificate of .... that a certificate of my birth is not available). (He is not employed or,— is by occupation employed at .... by ....).

(6a. Said infant is not a member of any armed forces or merchant marine nor engaged in or inducted for any military or naval service. He is not registered and not required to be registered under the United States Selective Service Act. (Or— He is duly registered under the said name of .... with Local Board No. ... of United States Selective Service, at .... Street, ..., New York.))

7. The said infant is now a citizen of the United States of America and has been such since (his birth).

8. The said infant is single and has never been married.

9. The said infant has never been convicted of any crime (except ....).

10. There are no judgments or liens of record against the said infant or against any property in his name. There is no ac-

tion or proceeding pending to which he is a party. He has never been adjudicated a bankrupt. In fact, no proceeding in bankruptcy has ever been instituted by or against him in any court or before any officer of the state or of the United States nor has said infant at any time made an assignment for the benefit of creditors. There are no claims, demands, liabilities, or obligations on a written instrument or otherwise against the said infant or to which the said infant is a party. The said infant has no creditors and no person will be adversely affected or prejudiced in any way by the proposed change of name.

11. The grounds of this application are the following: *(Set forth grounds of application, as for instance:* As aforesaid, the said infant resides with petitioner and his wife at their home at .... Street, ..., New York, and he has so resided since ...., 19.... Also as aforesaid, the parents of the said infant are both deceased, and on the said last mentioned date, petitioner brought the said infant to live at his home with the intention of bringing him up and educating him. Petitioner did this because he was a cousin to the father of the said infant and always very friendly with both of his parents. The said infant was left destitute and without means and, if petitioner had not taken him, he would have been placed in some foster home. Petitioner now desires that the family name of the said infant be changed to the family name of petitioner. The said infant has always been known by the name of .... and has always and will always be treated as the own child of petitioner. Petitioner and his wife have no children of their own and have no expectancy of any. They are very fond of the said infant and will always care for him. He will soon be of school age and petitioner desires to register him as his own child and by the name of ......
...... It is thought that a formal change of the name of the said infant to that of .... would save much embarrassment for the child as he grows older and be very advantageous under the circumstances. Petitioner and his wife would formally adopt the said infant as their own child were it not for the fact that peti-

tioner's father, ... of ...., New York, is opposed to such adoption and has forbidden the same. In fact, he is so strongly opposed to such adoption that he has stated that he would refuse to recognize petitioner as a son if the adoption were effected.)

WHEREFORE, it is respectfully submitted that the name of the said infant .... should be changed to that of .... and that this court grant an order effecting such change, for which relief no previous application has been made.

Dated, ..., 19....

....
Attorney for Petitioner

Office Address

....
Telephone Number ....

(Verification)

SECTION 62   FORM 1

Notice of Petition to Change Name of Infant

. . . . Court—. . . . . County

In the Matter of the Application for
the Change of Name
of
. . . . ,
an infant,
By . . . . , his general
guardian (*or*, guardian of his per
son, next friend, father, mother)

Notice of Petition

Index No. . . . .

PLEASE TAKE NOTICE, that the annexed petition will be pre-
sented to a special term of the . . . . Court, ...
County, appointed to be held at the Courthouse at . . . . ,
New York, on the . . . . . . day of . . . . , 19. . ., at the open-
ing of court on that day or as soon thereafter as counsel can be
heard, and that an application will then and there be made for
an order of the court directing a change of the name of the said
. . . . , an infant, to the name of . . . . , pursuant to
the provisions of Article 6 of the Civil Rights Law of the State
of New York and that the petitioner will then and there apply
for such other incidental or proper relief as the court may deem
just and proper.

Dated, ..., 19....

....
Attorney for petitioner

Office Address

....
Telephone Number ....

To ....

Father *(or, mother, general guardian,*
guardian of person, etc., of said infant).

SECTION 63   FORM 1

Order Changing Name; General Form[1]

> At a Special Term, Part ..., of
> the .... Court of the
> State of New York, held in
> and for the County of ......
> ...., at the Courthouse,
> .... Streets, ...
> ......, City of ....,
> N. Y., on the .... day of
> ...., 19....

In the Matter of the Application
of
....
for leave to change his name to
....

Order

Index No. ....

On reading and filing the petition of .... verified
the ...... day of ...., 19..., praying for a change
of name of the petitioner (or,— of the above named infant)

[1] **Order.**—Civil Rights Law § 63 was
amended by L. 1970, Ch. 314, eff. Sept.
1, 1970, to read as follows:

"If the court to which the petition
is presented is satisfied thereby, or
by the affidavit and certificate presented therewith, that the petition is
true, and that there is no reasonable
objection to the change of name proposed, and if the petition be to
change the name of an infant, that
the interests of the infant will be
substantially promoted by the change,
the court shall make an order authorizing the petitioner to assume
the name proposed on a day specified therein, not less than thirty days
after the entry of the order. The
order shall further recite the date
and place of birth of the applicant and, if the applicant was born
in the state of New York, such order
shall set forth the number of his
birth certificate or that no birth certificate is available. The order shall
be directed to be entered and the
papers on which it was granted to
be filed within ten days thereafter
in the clerk's office of the county in
which the petitioner resides if he be
an individual, or in the office of the
clerk of the civil court of the city of
New York if the order be made by
that court. Such order shall also direct the publication, at least once,
within twenty days after entry of the
order, in a designated newspaper in
the county in which the order is
directed to be entered, of a notice
in substantially the following form:

it being requested that he be permitted to assume the name of .... in the place and stead of his present name, (and notice of this application having been given to ...., (the father) of the above named ...., an infant, by the personal service of a copy of the notice of application herein, dated ...., 19..., upon him at ...., New York, on ...., 19..., and such notice appearing to the court to be sufficient notice of this application, further notice hereby is dispensed with;) and the court being satisfied that the petition is true and it appearing from the petition and the court being satisfied that there is no reasonable objection to the change of name proposed (and it further appearing that the applicant (or,— infant) was born on ...., 19..., at .... and that the certificate of his birth issued by (the Commissioner or local Board of Health) bears Number ...... (or,— and that a certificate of his birth is not available;) [and it further duly appearing that the applicant (or— said infant) is not registered and not required to be registered under the provisions of the United States Selective Service Act (or,— is duly registered under said name of .... with Local Board No. ... of United States Selective Service at ...., New York); and it further duly appearing that the interests of the said infant will be substantially promoted by the change;]

Now, on Motion of ...., attorney for the said petitioner, it is ordered that

1. ...., (born on ...., 19..., at ...., with birth certificate Number ... issued by Department of Health of .... (or,— with no birth certificate available)) be and he hereby is authorized to assume the name of .... in place and stead of his present name upon

Notice is hereby given that an order entered by the ...... court, ... county, on the .... day of ...., bearing Index Number ...., a copy of which may be examined at the office of the clerk, located at ......, in room number .... grants me the right, effective on the .... day of ...., to assume the name of .... My present address is ....; the date of my birth is ....; the place of my birth is ....; my present name is ...."

Form.—This form has been revised to conform to the law as amended and supersedes Section 63, Form 1 in the main volume.

complying with the provisions of Article 6 of the Civil Rights Law and of this order.

2. This order shall be entered and the petition upon which it was granted be filed within ten days from the date hereof in the office of the clerk of the county in which the petitioner resides (or in the office of the clerk of the Civil Court of the City of New York if the order be made by that court).

3. At least once within twenty days after the entry of this order, a notice shall be published in the ....
......, a newspaper published in the County of ...., New York, in substantially the following form:

Notice is hereby given that an order entered by the ....
court, ... county, on the .... day of ....,
bearing Index Number ...., a copy of which may be examined at the office of the clerk, located at ...., in room number ...., grants me the right, effective on the ...... day of ...., to assume the name of ....
My present address is ....; the date of my birth is ....; the place of my birth is ....; my present name is ....

4. Within forty days of the making of this order, proof of such publication by affidavit shall be filed with the clerk of (The Supreme Court in) the County of ....

5. (A copy of this order and the papers upon which it is based shall be served by (registered) mail upon the Chairman of Local Board No. ... of the United States Selective Service at which the said applicant (or,— infant) is registered for selective service (as above set forth), within twenty days after entry of this order, and proof of such service shall be filed with the clerk of (this court in) the said County of ....
within ten days after such service).

6. Following filing of the petition and entry of order as hereinbefore directed, the publication of such order and the filing of proof of publication thereof, and the service of a copy of said order and said papers as hereinbefore directed, and, on and after the .... day of ...., 19..., the petitioner (or,— said infant) ...., shall be known as and by the name of ...., which he is hereby authorized to assume and by no other name.

7. (Certified copy of this order shall not be issued until proof of compliance with the above provisions has been filed with the clerk of this court.)

Enter.

....
(Print Name)
Justice .... Court
County of ....

SECTION 63   FORM 4

Order Changing Name; Directing Change of Name of Infant[1]

> At a Special Term, Part II, of
> the Civil Court of the City
> of New York, at the Court-
> house thereof, ...
> Street, in the Borough of
> Manhattan, County of New
> York, City and State of New
> York, on the . . . . . . day of
> . . . . , 19. . . .

In the Matter of the Application of
. . . .
in behalf of her Child
. . . .
for leave to change her name to
. . . .

Upon reading and filing the annexed petition of . . . .
dated the . . . . . . day of . . . . , 19. . . , in behalf of her
child, ... , an infant four (4) years of age, who was
born in New York, N. Y., on . . . . , 19. . . , birth certificate No. . . . . . . , praying for leave to change the name of
said infant to . . . . , and upon the petition of . . . . ,
husband of . . . . , and a citizen of the United States,
consenting to the application for said change of name, and it
appearing that there are no reasonable objections to the proposed change of name, and the Court being satisfied that the
said petition is true;

Now, on the motion of . . . . , attorney for said petitioner, it is ordered that

1. . . . . be and she hereby is authorized to assume
the name of . . . . in place and stead of her present

---

1 **Form.**—This form has been revised
to comply with the law as amended,
1970, and supersedes Section 63, Form
4, in the main volume.
  See also Section 63, Form 1, N. 1,
supra.

name after the ...... day of ...., 19..., upon compliance with Article 6 of the Civil Rights Law and the provisions of this order.

2. This order shall be entered and the petition upon which it was granted be filed within ten days from the date hereof in the office of the clerk of this Court in the County of ...., and at least once within twenty days after the entry of the order a notice of this order shall be published in the ...., a newspaper published in the County of ...., in substantially the following form:

Notice is hereby given that an order entered by the .... court, ... county, on the ...... day of ...., bearing Index Number ...., a copy of which may be examined at the office of the clerk, located at ...., in room number ....., grants me the right, effective on the ..... day of ...., to assume the name of .... My present address is ....; the date of my birth is ....; the place of my birth is ......; my present name is ....

3. Within forty days of the making of this order, proof of such publication by affidavit shall be filed with the clerk of this Court in the County of ....; and

4. After such requirements are complied with, the petitioner shall, on and after the ...... day of ...., 19..., be known by the name of ...., which she is hereby authorized to assume, and by no other name, (and it is further ordered that sufficient cause having been shown, notice to .... is dispensed with.)

ENTER,

....
(Print name)
Judge of the Civil Court
of the City of New York
County of ....

SECTION 64   FORM 1

Certificate of Compliance With Order for Change of Name [1]

The undersigned, Clerk of the .... Court, in which the foregoing order was entered does hereby certify that said order has been complied with in that the papers on which it was granted were filed in the office of the undersigned within 10 days of the making of said order; that within 20 days after the entry of said order, publication thereof was made as directed by said order and that within 40 days after the making of said order an affidavit of publication thereof as aforesaid was filed in the office of the undersigned.

This certificate is made pursuant to Section 64 of the Civil Rights Law of the State of New York.

Dated: ...., 19...

....
Clerk

[1] **Effect.**—Civil Rights Law § 64 provides:

"If the order shall be fully complied with, and within forty days after the making of the order, an affidavit of the publication thereof shall be filed in the office in which the order is entered, the petitioner shall, on and after the day specified for that purpose in the order, be known by the name which is thereby authorized to be assumed, and by no other name. If the surname of a parent be changed as provided in this article, any minor child of such parent at the time of such change may thereafter assume such changed surname.

"Upon compliance with the order and the filing of the affidavit of the publication, as provided in this section, the clerk of the court in which the order has been entered shall certify that the order has been complied with. Such certification shall appear on the original order and on any certified copy thereof and shall be entered in the clerk's minutes of the proceeding."

COMMON LAW

Alice W. Smith v. United States Casualty Company
197 N.Y. 420

Change of name -- when name may be lawfully changed without application to the court.

(Argued January 18, 1910; decided February 8, 1910.)

. . . The question presented by this appeal, therefore, is whether at common law a man can change his name in good faith and for an honest purpose, by adopting a new one and for many years transacting his business and holding himself out to his friends and aquaintances thereunder, with their acquiescence and recognition? A change of name by proceedings under the statute is not involved.

As the common law rests so largely upon the customs of the people, it is often necessary to search the history of remote periods, both in England and in this country, in order to learn its full scope and meaning. While the legal name of a person now consists of a given name, or one given by his parents, and a surname, or one descending from them, history shows that this was not always the case. In the early life of all races surnames were unknown, while given names have been used from the most distant times to identify and distinguish a particular individual from his fellows. In England surnames were unknown until about the tenth century and they did not come into general use or become hereditary until many years later. (8 Nelson's Encyc. 386.) At first they were used, sometimes for an easy method of identification and at others from accident, caprice, taste and a multitude of other causes. Mr. Bardsley in his History of English Surnames gives thousands of instances of change through selection, the action of neighbors in applying descriptive epithets, the use of nicknames and pet names and the gradual development through circumstances and the necessity of identification as population increased. Thus the son of John or Peter became known as John's son or Peter's son and finally as Johnson or Peterson, aside from his given name. It is well known that the word meaning "son" in different languages, such as Fitz and Mac, was prefixed to the Christian name of the father to give the son a surname and "O" to give one to the grandson, and thus we have the names FitzGerald, MacDonough, O'Brien and many others. The place of birth or residence, the name of an estate, the business pursued, physical characteristics, mental or moral qualities and the like, were turned into surnames. It is to be noted, however, that the surname in its origin was not as a rule inherited from the father, but either adopted by the son, or bestowed upon him by the people of the community where he lived. (Dudgeon's Origin of Surnames, 252.) Father and son did not always have the same surname and it was not regarded as important, for both frequently had more than one. Coke wrote in the forepart of the seventeenth century: "Special heed is to be taken of the name of baptism as a man cannot have two, though he may have divers surnames." (Coke Lit. [1st Am. ed.] 3, a. m.)

So in Button v. Wrightman (Popham's Reports, 56), the learned chief justice and reporter said: "Anciently men took most commonly their surnames from their places of habitation, especially men of estates, and artisans often took their names from their arts, but yet the law is not so precise in the case of surnames and, therefore, a grant made by or to John, son and heir of I. C. or filio juniori, I. S. is good, but for the Christian name, this always ought to be perfect."

Camden mentions a man with eight sons, each with a different surname and not one with that of his father. (Camden's Remains, 141.) In a scholarly opinion by Chief Judge Daly, to which we are much indebted, many instances are mentioned where the color of the individual as White, Black or Brown, his height or strength, as Little, Long, Hardy or Strong; mental or moral attributes as Good, Wiley, Gay, Moody or Wise, fixed the surname. (In re Snook, 2 Hilt. 566.)

The learned judge continued: "The surname was frequently a chance appellation, assumed by the individual himself, or given to him by others, for some marked characteristic, such as his mental, moral or bodily qualities, some peculiarity or defect, or for some act he had done which attached to his descendants, while sometimes it did not. * ** It was in this way that the bulk of our surnames, that are not of foreign extraction, originated and became permanent. They grew into general use, without any law commanding their adoption, or prescribing any course or mode respecting them; * * * but though the custom is widespread and universal for all males to bear the names of their parents, there is nothing in law prohibiting a man from taking another name if he chooses. There is no penalty or punishment for so doing, nor any consequence growing out of it, except so far as it may lead to or cause a confounding of his identity."

The history of literature and art furnishes many examples of men who abandoned the name of their youth and chose the one made illustrious by their writings or paintings. Melanchthon's family name was Schwartzerde, meaning black-earth, but as soon as his literary talents developed and he began to forecast his future he changed it to the classical synonym by which he is known to history.

Rembrandt's father had the surname Gerretz, but the son, when his tastes broadened and his hand gained in cunning, changed it to Van Ryn on account of its greater dignity.

A predecessor of Honoré de Balzac was born a Guez, which means beggar, and grew to manhood under that surname. When he became conscious of his powers as a writer he did not wish his works to be published under that humble name, so he selected the surname Balzac from an estate that he owned. He made the name famous, and the later Balzac made it immortal.

Voltaire, Molière, Dantè, Petrarch, Richelieu, Loyola, Erasmus and Linnaeus were assumed names. Napoleon Bonaparte changed his name after his amazing victories had lured him toward a crown and he wanted a grander name to aid his daring aspirations. The Duke of Wellington was not by blood a Wellesley but a Colley, his grandfather, Richard Colley, having assumed the name of a relative names Wesley, which was afterward expanded to Wellesley. (S. Baring-Gould's Famous Names and Their Story, 391.) This author in his chapter on Changed Names gives many examples of men well known to history who changed their names by simply adopting a new one in place of the old.

Mr. Walsh, in his Handbook of Literary Curiosities, makes an interesting statement at page 778: "Authors and actors know the value of a mouth-filling name. Herbert Lythe becomes famous as Maurice Barrymore, Bridget O'Toole charms an audience as Rosa d'Erina, John H. Broadribb becomes Henry Irving. Samuel L. Clemens and Charles R. Browne attract attention under the eccentric masks of Mark Twain and Artemus Ward. John Rowlands would never have become a great explorer unless he had first changed his name to Henry M. Stanley. James B. Matthews and James B. Taylor might have remained lost among the mass of magazine contributors but for their cunning in dropping the James and standing forth as Brander Matthews and Bayard Taylor. Would Jacob W. Reid have succeeded as well as Whitelaw Reid?'' While some of these names were merely professional pseudonyms, others were adopted as the real name and in time became the only name of the person who assumed it.

Many other instances of voluntary change of name, both given and surname, might be added, but we will mention only two more. In Larke's ''General Grant and His Campaigns'' (p.13) it is stated, and the fact is well known, that ''General Grant's baptismal name was Hiram Ulysses and he bore that appellation until he was appointed a cadet at West Point. General Hamer, who nominated him for a cadetship, by some means got his name mixed up with that of his brother. He was, therefore, appointed as 'Ulysses Sidney Grant,'' and that name once so recorded on the books of the military academy could not be changed. He was baptized into the military school as U. S. Grant and he has ever since been thus designated.''

Another instance, equally well established by current history, is that of President Cleveland, who had the baptismal name of Stephen G. Cleveland. After he entered his teen he omitted the word ''Stephen'' and assumed the name of Grover Cleveland, by which he was known throughout his distinguished career.

Out of the groundwork of custom, as shown by the early history of the subject, the common law sprang and was gradually developed. The ancient custom was for the son to adopt a surname at will, regardless of that borne by his father, and the practice, continued occasionally until the present time, has extended to the given name also. If the insurance policy in question had been issued, under the same circumstances, to General Grant or President Cleveland, would it have been valid? Indeed, it may well be asked, would it have been valid if issued to either of those noted men, had it followed the name given at birth instead of the one acquired by adoption and by which they were known while filling the most exalted positions and will be known for all time?

There are but few decisions directly in point, although there are many dicta by eminent judges recognizing as an established rule that a man may change his name, Christian, surname, or both, without resort to legal proceedings.

In <u>Doe</u> ex <u>dem. Luscombe</u> v. <u>Yates</u> (5 Barn. & Ald. 544) there was a devise of an estate to one Manning, provided within three years after entering into possession he should procure his name "to be altered and changed to my name of Luscombe, by act or acts of Parliament, or some other effectual way for that purpose," and in default of thus changing his name the devise was to become void. Without applying to Parliament for an act of relief or to the king for a license, he adopted the name of Luscombe, and used it for all purposes to the exclusion of his former surname. It was held that he was entitled to retain the estate, the court through Chief Justice Abbott saying: "A name assumed by the voluntary act of a young man at his outset into life, adopted by all who knew him and by which he is constantly called, becomes for all purposes that occur to my mind as much and effectually his name as if he had obtained an act of Parliament to confer it upon him."

In Laflin & Rand Co. v. Steytler (146 Pa. St. 434) an act authorizing the formation of limited partnerships required the articles of association to "set forth the full names of" the members. The adopted name of one of the partners was given as his full name, and an attempt was made to hold the special partners liable as general partners for that reason. The court defeated the effort and, in discussing the question, said: "A man's given name is the designation by which he is distinctively known in the community. Custom gives him the family name of his father and such praenomina as his parents choose to put before it, and appropriate circumstances may require Sr. or Jr. as a further constituent part, but all this is only a general rule from which the individual may depart if he chooses. The legislature in 1852 provided a mode of changing the name, but that act was in affirmance and aid of the common law, to make a definite point of time at which a change shall take effect. Without the aid of that act, a man may change his name or names, first or last, and when his neighbors and the community have acquiesced and recognized him by his new designation, that becomes his name."

The case last cited was soon followed by another in the same court to the effect that the requirement of the statute as to "full names" was "met by giving the names in the form habitually used by those persons in business and by which they are generally known in the community." (Gearing v. Carroll, 151 Pa. St. 79, 84. See, also, England v. New York Pub. Co., 8 Daly, 375, 381; Cooper v. Burr, 45 Barb. 9, 34; Bell v. Sun Printing & Pub. Co., 42 N.Y. Super. Ct. 567, 569; City Council v. King, 4 McCord, 487; Hommel v. Devinney, 39 Mich. 522;

Binfield v. State, 15 Neb. 484; Linton v. First National Bank, 10 Fed. Rep. 894; The King v. Inhabitants of Billingshurst, 3 Maule & S. 250.)

The elementary writers are uniform in laying down the rule that at common law a man may change his name at will.

Mr. Throckmorton, in his article on Names in the Cyclopedia of Law and Procedure, says: "It is a custom for persons to bear the surname of their parents, but it is not obligatory. A man may lawfully change his name without resort to legal proceedings, and for all purposes the name thus assumed will constitute his legal name just as much as if he had borne it from birth." (29 Cyc. 271.)

So a writer in the American & English Encyclopedia of Law says: "At common law a man may lawfully change his name, or by general usage or habit acquire another name than that originally borne by him, and this without the intervention of either the sovereign, the courts, or Parliament; and the common law, unless changed by statute, of course obtains in the United States." (21 Am. & Eng. Encyc. of Law [2d ed.], 311.)

"One may legally name himself, or change his name, or acquire a name by reputation, general usage, and habit." (2 Fiero Sp. Pro. [2d ed.] 847.)

The subject is not affected by the various statutes, commencing in 1847 and continuing with some expansion and changes to the present time, whereby a change of name is authorized by judicial proceedings. (L. 1847, ch. 464; Code Civ. Pro. §§ 2410-2415.) As was said by the Supreme Court of Pennsylvania of a similar statute in that state, this legislation is simply in affirmance and aid of the common law to make a definite point of time when the change shall take effect. (Laflin & Rand Co. v. Steytler, supra.) It does not repeal the common law by implication or otherwise, but gives an additional method of effecting a change of name. The statutory method has some advantages, because it is speedy, definite and a matter of record, so as to be easily proved even after the death of all contemporaneous witnesses. In one respect, however, the statute may limit the common-law right, in that it provides that on and after the day specified in the order of the court for the change to take effect, the applicant shall "be known by the name which is thereby authorized to be assumed, and by no other name." (Code Civ. Pro. § 2415.) It may well be, therefore, that after a man has acquired a name by judicial decree, he cannot acquire another without resorting to the courts. [See also 124 N.Y.S. 989 for a history of Jewish names; see also in re Romm, 77 D. & C. 481 (Pa. 1952)]

Appendix D

CASE CITATIONS

Throughout this book the reader will have noted that the cases which are used to illustrate the legal points involved are identified by a reference to what is known as a citation. These citations relate to the source books where the cases are printed in full and which the reader may turn to, provided, of course, that he has access to them. They will generally be found in large public libraries and in libraries which are used primarily by lawyers. A brief explanation of these sources, or "reports", may be helpful to the reader.

We have, wherever possible, given two sources for each case: one source is the official state reports and the other is the National Reporter System. The official state reports are designated by, first, a number indicating the volume in the series; secondly, the abbreviation of the state or state court; and thirdly, the page number in the volume. The National Reporter System is a series of books which are planned on a geographical basis, and which contain the opinions of the courts in a particular area, which may cover a number of states. In this system there are the Atlantic Reporter, the North Eastern Reporter, the North Western Reporter, the Pacific Reporter, the South Eastern Reporter, the Southern Reporter, the South Western Reporter. There is also the Supreme Court Reporter, designated by "U.S.", the Federal Reporter, the Federal Supplement, the New York Supplement, the New York Miscellaneous Reports, and the New York Appellate Division Reports, the last two

Designated respectively as "Misc." and "A.D." Each state may have, also, in addition to its official reports, unofficial reports with various titles. The reader is advised to consult with a librarian in case of difficulty. It may be mentioned that some of the reports will have after them the indication "(2)" or "(2nd)" which means the second series of that set of reports.

MAIDEN NAME BILLS

The following bills were offered to the New York legislature to provide women with equal consideration under the law with regard to the use of their names.

STATE OF NEW YORK

1511

1973–1974 Regular Sessions

IN ASSEMBLY

January 16, 1973

Introduced by Mr. OLIVIERI—read once and referred to the Committee on Judiciary

AN ACT

to amend the domestic relations law, in relation to retention or change of name at marriage

The People of the State of New York, represented in Senate and Assembly, do enact as follows:

1   Section 1. Subdivision one of section fifteen of the domestic rel-

2 ations law, as last amended by chapter one hundred two of the laws of

3 nineteen hundred sixty-five, is hereby amended to read as follows:

4   1. It shall be the duty of the town or city clerk when an application

5 for a marriage license is made to him to require each of the contracting

6 parties to sign and verify a statement or affidavit before such clerk or

7 one of his deputies, containing the following information. From [the

8 groom] *each applicant*: Full name of [husband] *applicant*, place of

9 residence, age, occupation, place of birth, name of father, country of

EXPLANATION — Matter in *italics* is new; matter in brackets [ ] is old law to be omitted.
C

2

1 birth, maiden name of mother, country of birth, number of marriage[.

2 From the bride: Full name of bride, place of residence, age, occupa-

3 tion, place of birth, name of father, country of birth, maiden name of

4 mother, country of birth, number of marriage] *and name that appli-*

5 *cant chooses to retain or assume upon marriage.* The said clerk shall

6 also embody in the statement if either or both of the applicants have

7 been previously married, a statement as to whether the former hus-

8 band or husbands or the former wife or wives of the respective appli-

9 cants are living or dead and as to whether either or both of said appli-

10 cants are divorced persons, if so, when and where and against whom

11 the divorce or divorces were granted and shall also embody therein a

12 statement that no legal impediment exists as to the right of each of the

13 applicants to enter into the marriage state. The town or city clerk is

14 hereby given full power and authority to administer oaths and may

15 require the applicants to produce witnesses to identify them or either

16 of them and may examine under oath or otherwise other witnesses as

17 to any material inquiry pertaining to the issuing of the license, and if

18 the applicant is a divorced person the clerk may also require the pro-

19 duction of a certified copy of the decree of the divorce, or proof of an

20 existing marriage of parties who apply for a license to be used for a

21 second or subsequent ceremony; provided, however, that in cities of

22 the first class the verified statements and affidavits may be made

23 before any regular clerk of the city clerk's office designated for that

24 purpose by the city clerk.

25 § 2. Such law is hereby amended by adding thereto a new section,

26 to be section fifty-one, to read as follows:

3

1   § 51. *Retention or change of name at marriage. When marrying,*

2 *a person may retain his or her name or may adopt as his or her name*

3 *the name of the spouse or a combination of the names of both parties.*

4 *The post-marriage name chosen by each applicant for a marriage*

5 *license pursuant to section fifteen of this act shall become the name of*

6 *such applicant upon marriage.*

7   § 3. This act shall take effect immediately.

STATE OF NEW YORK

1535

1973-1974 Regular Sessions

IN SENATE

January 22, 1973

Introduced by Sen. GORDON—read twice and ordered printed, and when printed to be committed to the Committee on Judiciary

AN ACT

To amend the domestic relations law, in relation to resumption of the use of maiden name by a woman in certain cases

The People of the State of New York, represented in Senate and Assembly, do enact as follows:

1   Section 1. The domestic relations law is hereby amended by add-

2 ing thereto a new section, to be section two hundred forty-a, to read

3 as follows:

4   *§ 240-a. Judgment or decree; additional provision. In any*

5 *action or proceeding brought under the provisions of this chapter*

6 *wherein all or part of the relief sought is divorce or annulment of*

7 *a marriage any interlocutory or final judgment or decree shall con-*

8 *tain, as a part thereof, a provision that the woman may resume the*

9 *use of her maiden name.*

10   § 2. This act shall take effect on the thirtieth day after it shall

11 have become law.

.

BIBLIOGRAPHY

16 La Abogada International (Spring 1972). Articles on the status of women in Germany, Mexico, Nigeria, Thai, Canada, with reference to change of name rights.

Adamic, Louis. What's Your Name? New York: Harper, 1942.

American Civil Liberties Union. ''Right of Married Women to Retain or Regain Their Birth Names.'' (Position Paper) 1972.

38 American Jurisprudence, Name, § 28-35. A legal encyclopedia that covers all aspects of change of name law.

10 American Jurisprudence, Legal Forms. A form book that ties in with American Jurisprudence and other units of the Lawyers Cooperative Publishing Co. ''Total Client'' service.

14 American Jurisprudence Practice and Pleading Forms. Form Nos. 14:891 et seq. cover change of name. See previous entry.

35 American Law Reports 416 (1925). Correct name of married woman. Provides exhaustive references to case law. Also a unit of ''Total Client'' service.

110 American Law Reports 219 (1937). Duty and discretion of court in passing upon petition to change name of individual.

44 American Law Reports, 2d 1156, at 1171 (1955). Use of adopted or assumed name by individual, etc.

53 American Law Reports 2d 914 (1957). Rights and remedies of parents inter se with respect to the names of their children.

Assumed names, 29 Chicago-Kent L. Rev. 282 (1951).

Bentham, What's in a name? 115 Just. P. 616 (1951).

Brown, Emerson, Falk, Freedman, The Equal Rights Amendment: A Constitutional basis for equal rights for women, 80 Yale L. J. 871, at 940 (1971).

Cantor, Change of name in Western Australia, 30 Aust. L. J. 289 (1956).

Carlsson, Surnames of married women and legitimate children, 17 New York Law Forum 552 (1971).

Changing one's name in Ontario, 19 Faculty L. Rev. 103 (1961).

65 Corpus Juris Secundum, Names. A legal encyclopedia that covers all aspects of change of name law. A unit of the West Publishing Co. For older cases consult Corpus Juris. West also publishes a great many state encyclopedias.

Daniell, Law relating to names: "he who steals my good name," 31. N. Z. L. J. 358 (1958).

Domestic relations: change of minor's surname: parental rights in minor's surname (Sobel v. Sobel -- N.J.) (Marshall v. Marshall -- Miss), 44 Cornell L. Q. 144 (1958).

Donlan, What's in a name? 41 Title News 4 (March 1962).

Eder, Right to choose a name, 8 Am. J. Comp. L. 502 (1959).

Effect of violation of assumed name statutes on enforcement of contracts, 27 Chicago-Kent L. Rev. 327 (1949), 44 Ill. L. Rev. 720 (1949).

Fictitious name statute, 5 S. D. L. Rev. 133 (1960).

Fictitious names, 18 So. Calif. L. Rev. 70 (1944).

Foster, Idem sonans, 29 Title News 33 (Oct. 1950).

Hughes, And then there were two, 23 Hastings L. J. 233 (1971).

Injunction -- surname of child (Mark v. Kahn -- Mass) (Solomon v. Solomon -- Ill), 34 Chicago-Kent L. Rev. 313 (1956).

Josling, Change of Name, 8th ed. London: Oyez, 1967.

Kahoe, Non-profit corporations' names, 21 Clev. St. L. Rev. 114 (1972).

Kanowitz, Leo. Women and the Law, the Unfinished Revolution. Univ. of New Mexico Press, 1969, p. 41-46.

Kittner, Married women -- change of name, 16 N. Car. L. Rev. 187 (1938).

Lester, What's in a name, 5 Bus. L. Rev. 19 (1958).

Linell, Anthony. The Law of Names, Public, Private, and Corporate. London: Butterworth, 1938.

Locke, Change of name following a divorce, 25 Manitoba Bar News 24 (1953).

Lund and Healy, Sex discrimination, in 1971 Annual Survey of Massachusetts Law (1972), p. 562, at 570.

McClintock, Fictitious business name legislation -- modernizing California's pioneer statute, 19 Hastings L. J. 1349 (1968).

Modern Legal Forms, 6161-6680. A unit of the West system. See the entry for Corpus Juris Secundum.

Morris, Middle initials, 37 Dicta 361 (1960).

Nichols, Cyclopedia of Legal Forms Annotated, §7.00-7.985.

Noye: And whose little girl are you? . . ., 2 San Fernando Valley Law Rev. p. 63, at 70 (1972-73).

Oka, What's in a name, Christian Science Monitor, Sept. 7, 1972, p. 1. French judge refused to change name of adopted boy to that of his new parents, Trognon, as it was a "ridiculous name."

Partridge, Eric, Name into Word. Freeport, N.Y. Books for Libraries, Reprint of 1950 ed.

Plotkin and Most, Use of personal names as unfair competition, 41 Los Angeles Bar Bull. 266 (April 1966).

Powell-Smith, Change of name problems, 116 New Law J. 1027 (1966).

Rider, Legal protection of the manifestations of individual personality -- the identity indicia, 33 S. Calif. L. Rev. 31 (1959).

Right to change one's name, 5 J. of Family Law 220 (1965).

Simmons, Change of names, 113 L. J. 212 (1963).

So you'd like a new name, New York Post, Dec. 26, 1972, p. 8.

Spiro, Name of a married woman, 66 South African Law J. 189 (1949).

Status of women, 20 Am. J. Comp. L, (Fall 1972). The law in Great Britain, Sweden, Norway, France, Soviet Union, Israel, Senegal, including references to change of name.

Stewart, George R., American Place-Names. Fairlawn, N.J.: Oxford University Press, 1970.

-----------------, Names on the Land, Boston: Houghton Mifflin, Co., 1945.

Taylor, Charlene M. and Stuart Herzog. Impact Study of the Equal Rights Amendment -- Subject: The Arizona Constitution and Statutes. Tucson, Ariz., 1973. 91 leaves.

Thimmesch, The sexual equality amendment, New York Times Magazine, June 24, 1973, p. 8, at 9.

Treece, Some qualifications on everyman's absolute right to use his own name in business, 46 Tex. L, Rev. 436 (1968).

Wallach, Comparative legal status of American and Soviet women, 5 Valparaiso Univ. L, Rev. 438, at 451 (1971).

Waugh, Fem lib strikes again, Christian Science Monitor, May 14, 1973, p. 15.

What's in a name, 87 Time 81 (May 1966).

Words and Phrases. A unit of the West system. See entry for Corpus Juris Secundum.

INDEX

Abbreviations, 36
Adoption, 14
Alien, 12
Assumed Name, 28-33

Bankruptcy, effect of, 20
Baptismal name, 2
Bibliography, 111
Birth records, 13
Blackstone, 46
Business names, 60

Children, 3-12
  Forms, 85
Common law, 3, 98
Conducting business under
  assumed name, 30-33
Corporate name, 60
Criminal complaint, 35-36

Damages,
  Misuse of name, 25-26
Deception, 25
Defamation, 41
Discretion of Court, 17
  Abuse of, 22-23
  Role of court as to, 57
Divorce (See also Married women)
  Resumption of name by, 14

Equal Rights Amendment, 59

Fictitious names, 28
First name, 38-40
Forgery, 29
Forms, 81-85

Homosexuals, 14

Idem sonans, 42-44

Identity, 34-44
Infants, 8-12
  Forms, 85
Initials, 38-40

Legal documents, 34

Married women, 45-59
  Blackstone on, 46
  Common law, 45 et seq.
  Credit, 56
  Critique of common law, 55
  Maiden name bills, 55, 106
  Separation, effect of, 15
  Voting, 51
Middle names, 38-40
Motive, 17-24
Mrs., 53
Ms., 53-54

Name, origin of (See specific
  headings), 1 et seq.
Naturalization, 18, 19, 54
Nom de plume, 28

Objections to petition
  Cabot, use of, 22

Petitions, 7
  Forms, 81
Publication, 7

Registration,
  Business name, 32-33
Residence, 8
Right of privacy, 25-27

Sex, change of, 13
Statutory method, 5-16

    Accuracy, 6
    Alien, 12
    Application, 7
    Children, 8
    Procedure, 5
    Publication, 7
    Residence, 8
    State constitutions and, 6
    Summary of state laws, 65
Subpoena, 38

Voting, 22

Wills, 36, 37

Yearbooks, 2